WHOLE LOTTA $$$ IN THIS MOFO

Book 1:
An Employer's Guide to Navigating Legalized Larceny Within American Healthcare

AN ANTHOLOGY PRESENTED BY:

DR. MADELINE SMITH

EMPOWERED PRESS

Published by: The Empowered Press

Las Cruces, New Mexico, USA

http://www.theempoweredpress.com

ISBN: 978-1-957430-08-9 (paperback)

ISBN: 978-1-957430-07-2 (hardback)

ISBN: 978-1-9574301-09-6 (ebook)

Library of Congress Control Number: 2022949487

For information:

The Empowered Press

publish@theempoweredpress.com

Cover design by Onur Aksoy

Onegraphica.com

To God, my husband Scottie, and my sweet boys: JR, Tate, and Ray

"People's indifference is the best breeding ground for corruption to grow."

— Delia Ferreira

PRESENTER'S NOTE

This is a work of nonfiction. While each chapter contains valuable, actionable information and insight for employers, this book is for informational purposes only. It is not meant to take the place of a qualified benefit advisor reviewing your actual data and strategy. This book is not intended as specific guidance or advice for what an employer should do with their health plan. Each employer group and its respective benefits plan is unique. If you need advice concerning your health plan, please seek out a qualified health plan advisor.

I set out on this anthology journey with two goals. First, I wanted to get real, authentic knowledge directly into the hands of employers, surpassing the layers of middlemen littering the health insurance industry. Second, I saw this as a unique opportunity to elevate the thought leaders I've encountered in the industry. In retrospect, while not every leader I hoped for is represented in these pages, I feel we met and exceeded both goals.

During the process, an ugly truth emerged. There is an alarming disproportion of men to women in this industry, and many women face a virtually impossible battle to get to leadership positions. The silver lining I discovered, though, was the men who make every effort to empower and elevate powerful women in this business. This is not unique to health insurance and employee benefits, but it's worth acknowledging so we can work together to combat it.

Every contributor in this anthology is not only an exceptional subject matter expert but should be seen as a brave change agent to be revered.

I hope the profanity in the book is not offensive. I found it necessary to share the raw, unfiltered, authentic rage many of us feel at the fact that Americans can't afford healthcare and employers are stuck with a bill they don't understand, with no idea how to fix it except to blame doctors.

What should be offensive is how corrupt and deceitful the industry can be, but that emotion is useless if we don't come together to create real change.

CONTENTS

FOREWORD

Have you ever seen a problem or circumstance and said, "Somebody should do something about this!" We all have said it and then promptly gone out and done nothing to rectify the problem or circumstance. We justify in our minds that the problem is too big and we're so small that there isn't anything we could do about it anyway. However, there are a select few individuals that see the problem or circumstance and think, "Somebody should do something about this, and if they won't, then I will." And they begin immediately down the path to find solutions to the problem or circumstance.

I am lucky to have met and become dear friends with one such "somebody." In the years I have known Madeline Smith, she has shown the world how much can be done by one soul determined to make a huge difference. She is a dedicated wife and a loving mother to three active boys. She is in law school at night because it's something she has always wanted to do. She volunteers with local nonprofits in her spare time. Dr. Smith has taken her passion for helping people through non-profit organizations to being a solutions-driven professional in the healthcare/benefits arena with the end consumer at the forefront. Up to this point, an arena mainly dominated by large insurance companies offering off-the-shelf primarily driven by Wall Street profits and returns. This has left business owners and HR professionals constantly scrambling to try and find the diamond in the rough in the pile of crap these companies offer.

Madeline has taken the industry and flipped it on its head. Not only will you learn more about how to provide real solutions to your company by reading and applying this book, but you will also begin to see a better way of being solutions-driven when it comes to your specific benefits needs.

To quote the "great philosopher" Captain Jack Sparrow, "The problem is not the problem; the problem is your attitude about the problem." Madeline's attitude about how to provide actual solutions that the world needs permeate throughout this book and shows why she is a leader in the space and is a force to be reckoned with.

Collin Bryce
Financial Professional/Business Consultant

Collin Bryce is a thought leader and innovator within the financial operations sector, with special experience in private equity, land acquisition and development, asset management, and insurance planning. His reputation for excellence is paired with his generosity for his larger community, making a difference in the world, and his love for his wife and four children.

CHAPTER 1
FOLLOW THE DAMN $$$

DR. MADELINE SMITH

Health insurance is perhaps the century's richest, most successful marketing scam turned acceptable practice.

———

WHEN I TOLD my family and friends that I was leaving my career as a social worker and moving into a health insurance role, most responses I got were stupefied. My husband was excited because we both thought it meant I would be less emotionally invested in my job than when I worked in non-profits (we were wrong!).

I guess the excitement my family had for me, thinking I could finally pay my bills, was canceled out by the feelings they had about insurance salespeople. They assumed I would promptly buy a brown leather briefcase and go door to door selling life/health policies (which I am not knocking, I owe a debt of gratitude to a few of those salespeople who taught me so much). But it's an understandable reaction. Insurance is seen by many who don't understand it as a scam. I would go from one of the most philanthropic, selfless careers to selling insurance. They weren't sure if they should share their congratulations or condolences.

The stories flowed in from friends and family on all sides: what to do, what not to do, what insurance everyone had, and what everyone hated about their insurance. One response from my mother still resonates with me after all these years. My mom knew me best, and I guess without me saying it, she knew I was getting into health insurance to help people, which was like her grandma. She said, "Your great-grandmother would be so proud of you."

Grandma Helen was the epitome of a grandmother at the turn of the century. She died when I was twelve years old, but I have vivid memories of her and the legacy she left. She was the wife of a farmer in a little town in Illinois. Born in 1902, she spent most of her 97 years on earth caring for others. My grandpa and his siblings remember people from town staying at their house to be cared for by her. They sometimes had to give up their rooms for them. She had no formal medical training; she was a phenomenal caregiver—a *Farmer's Almanac* type of healing was her specialty.

When I was young, I remember visiting her in her final years, relishing the legacy my family had in that town because of her. Our visits with her are some of my fondest childhood memories. Well, her chicken salad sandwiches, homemade strawberry jam, and freshly brewed sun tea.

Stories like that are less common today. Care in the home now happens primarily in temporary (or long-term) home care or hospice. I firmly believe that to understand where you are as a society or an individual, you must look at where you come from. Good, bad, or ugly. So, how did we get here?

It's important to acknowledge that the history of healthcare and health insurance are intertwined but not interchangeable. I would argue that the history of health insurance stemmed from the evolution of healthcare. It evolved out of necessity as the world of medicine was evolving. You may not know the history of health insurance, but you are a member of the system. Not just if you or your employees or family members have health insurance but if you've ever been to a doctor or hospital.

At the beginning of the twentieth century, healthcare and medicine were local, with little to no regulation. Care in the home was almost always the norm. There were hospitals, but they were few. Physicians often came to patients' homes, and people knew they would pay 100% of the doctor's fee. Folks didn't mind paying the fees (a fraction of what they are today) because the sooner they were healthy, the sooner they could return to work (either inside or outside the home). Illnesses were rarely treatable.

I'm intentionally digressing for a moment. Let's think about this. No matter how discouraging and confusing the health insurance world is (and sometimes healthcare itself), it has come so far when you consider that most illnesses today are treatable. For context, it wasn't until 1910 that the first drug treatment was available that could kill disease, and surgery became more common. Commercial insurance companies offered no health insurance. The carriers considered it but found no way to avoid taking losses.

The obstacles faced by insurance then are like the risks faced by insurance today. Most people don't consider these risks. One issue is adverse selection. This is the concept that the only people who seek insurance solutions are those who are sick and know they will need the protection, and the healthy folks won't purchase insurance. This leads to the likelihood that a carrier's premium would be lost to pay claims for unhealthy members who've bought the insurance out of necessity.

Another obstacle to early insurance was the concept of moral hazard. Here, this describes the phenomenon of members who now had insurance seeking unnecessary treatments simply because they had insurance. Insurance carriers still face these issues today but mitigate their impact or account for them in the pricing.

If you are reading this and thinking, "who would do that? I would never... My employees would never..." Consider a common scenario: have you ever met your deductible during the year and then realized you could have a procedure (useful perhaps, but not life or death) and have little or no out-of-pocket responsibility? You aren't alone. I will own it; I have done this. When I met my deductible after two weeks in the ICU and needed a non-emergency surgery later that year, I timed it just right. This is a commonly recognized occurrence within the medical world. As a plan year winds down and the new year approaches (when most health plan deductibles reset), there is a universal spike in claims. It is because everyone who met their deductibles is having tests, scans, labs, or procedures they couldn't afford earlier in the year. We don't think about this as consumers—we simply don't understand why insurance costs so much.

As much as we want to forget it, remember that insurance is a business. One with a gambling spirit, sure, but a business. Like any business, the goal is to make a profit, meaning taking in more than you pay out.

In the early 1900s, while European countries were forming national universal healthcare, the United States wasn't. We couldn't go in that direction because the insurance companies were hesitant about whether the model could be sustainable, and physicians weren't interested. The state of healthcare changed over the next couple of decades as technology advanced, and healthcare happened more and more outside the home. Medical care saw new programs, like accreditation organizations, and people became more concerned with cleanliness and medication protocol.

In 1929, the average annual income in the US was $1,916 (wow!), and about 5 percent was spent on medical expenses. Hospital care accounted for 14 percent of that. Baylor University Hospital in Dallas contracted with a group of schoolteachers, forever changing the face of healthcare. The agreement guaranteed the teachers up to twenty-one days of inpatient care in exchange for 50 cents a month. Throughout the Great Depression, prepaid health plans emerged with other hospitals. This was because they needed to find some guaranteed revenue to survive. Eight years later, over six hundred thousand members across the country belonged to such a plan. The healthcare insurance network system of American healthcare was born.[1]

In 1932, the American Hospital Association brought all these prepaid hospital plans together under the name "Blue Cross," which represented the first network of plans. State legislation supported their formation, allowing them to form a non-profit. With this, they could benefit from tax exemption and avoid insurance regulations. Soon, physicians became nervous about the Blue Cross network's role in their ability to keep clients and set their fees. They responded by forming their network insurance plan, covering physician services, and called it Blue Shield. They hoped this would prevent Blue Cross from entering the primary care business where the physicians were focused. Commercial insurers took notice and realized there might be a way to overcome the previously faced obstacles. They also figured there might be a profit if they insured a large population of relatively young, healthy Americans who had jobs.[2]

World War II played a unique role in the expansion of health insurance. Price and wage controls were implemented to prevent employers from offering higher wages when recruiting employees. Employers had to respond by finding unique ways to attract the most desirable employees. Health insurance was a new benefit, a perk that a new employer offered.

Health insurance, both by the Blues and commercial insurers, exploded, reaching over $20 million in 1940 and $142 million in 1950. The growth of Blue Cross and Blue Shield enrollment was aided by efforts of local philanthropic groups such as the Red Cross and various women's auxiliary groups. The overarching goal was to help individuals and families access this emerging plan to ease their financial stress and burden, ultimately aiding public health. There was no advertising, so to speak because they were non-profits and seen as charities. The message in publications like *Dallas Magazine* was that they were plans for the people, by the people.

Writings from that time reveal internal documents among hospital administrators, comparing their roles of leading a hospital to running a factory. We still see this mentality today in some hospital system management techniques where the administration is business-minded and far removed from the healthcare aspect of what they do.

Blue Cross and Blue Shield worked together at the request of the US government in the 1960s, forming the Blue Cross Blue Shield Association in 1982. Not until 1994 did the member organizations become for-profit. The history of Blue Cross Blue Shield (now Anthem) is crucial because it reminds us of the problem it aimed to solve.[3]

Other major carriers/networks you may recognize have varying histories. For example, Aetna goes back to the mid-1800s with its life and disability policies. They entered the medical insurance space in 1951.[4] Cigna's history began in 1792 with marine insurance, not offering medical insurance until 1942, when they were asked by the US

Army to insure a group of thirty men working on the Manhattan Project.[5] United Healthcare is the new kid on the block, forming in 1977.[6] These are the largest major medical corporations in the US, booking billions in profit each year.

Each of these insurance companies is also a network. We may not agree on many things, but we can all probably agree that insurance companies/networks do not make people healthier. They don't even increase our alive-ness scores. Unfortunately, we must admit they grant access to the people (doctors/nurses), places (hospitals and offices), and tools (medical equipment and prescriptions) that make us healthier and keep us alive. Those who say they "love their insurance" or "have great insurance" usually mean two things: one, it is afford-able, and two, their doctors are in their network.

How did health insurance carriers/networks insert themselves into the middle of the healthcare process? Because we let them. It is perhaps the century's richest, most successful marketing scam turned acceptable practice. It is like a social class system; having a well-known network logo on your card is a symbol. One could argue it is a social symbol of wealth.

If you would like to argue with me, I encourage you to visit a clinic that accepts insurance, Medicaid, and cash. In my pre-insurance days, I experienced it frequently while working in social work. At one time, I had a caseload of clients who depended on me and my agency for many things, including navigating the welfare system, the family justice system, etc. I often accompanied them on doctor visits with their infants or interviews to get their medical cards/food stamps. Again, this is not a political rant about the social welfare system. Believe me, if a person walks up to the registration desk at a clinic with a hard plastic Blue Cross Blue Shield card, the entire experience will be dramatically different than if that same person walks in with their medical card printed on paper or even a card with a logo the clinic doesn't recognize.

So, what does the network do for us? It plays on the psychology of the deal. Our brains love a bargain. It's like a going-out-of-business sale. We are all drawn to the discount section of our favorite stores. Usually, we can see the original price on the manufacturer's tag, so we can see if the discounted price represents 50 percent off. But what about what we can't see? Would we feel differently if the sign said 50 percent off and showed us the final price? Do we feel enough kinship with the store management to trust they gave us the discount they are promising? Is the shirt $50 and now only $25? Or was the shirt $25 all along? Either way, we are taking it on faith.

That's what a network discount represents. It's a discount on a made-up number. Most people don't realize what goes into the billed charge by the provider. There is a difference between a billed charge, what the insurance plan allows, what the plan pays, and the member's responsibility. Unless you're paying cash, it's not as simple as in 1929 when there was a straightforward transaction between patient and doctor. Now, providers and hospitals must consider several things when determining their costs, so they are prepared to negotiate with insurance companies. It's a far different practice than most service industries and their cost calculations.

I'm no economist, but let's say we were analyzing the cost model of a barber shop. The costs to consider would be shop rent, equipment, inventory, furniture, licenses, insurance, and marketing costs. The simple math is that a barber shop must charge customers more than it costs to serve them. In reverse, they must service enough clients to ideally make a profit. Cost considerations in healthcare are not so simple. Part of it is based on all the steps the medical providers need to follow to get paid. Still, part of it is also based on other considerations like the discounts they offer and the overall cost of customer acquisition.

Do you know where most dollars go in healthcare? Or how we got ourselves into such a complicated, messed-up system? I didn't know when I joined the health insurance industry, and there are still enormous black boxes I haven't been able to uncover (and probably never will).

Why does the US accept getting their knowledge about healthcare from insurance entities who don't do the work, while establishing monopolies over the flow of money? We don't do this in other areas of insurance. You don't call Geico or State Farm before you head to the car lot. You might pause and consider the cost of insurance before buying a brand-new Maserati or insuring your newly-driving sixteen-year-old son. But you likely do not pick the car lot based on your agent's suggestion. In either scenario, you'll probably proceed without a care for the insurance cost and are more focused on the cost of the car itself.

What about renter's or homeowner's insurance? I may be in the minority, but I shop for my homeowner's insurance *after* I pick the apartment/house, not before. I depend on my agent to suggest wind/hail deductibles and various limits, but they didn't dictate what homes I toured. When I got my first apartment, I did what any convincing know-it-all nineteen-year-old does; I went to my mentor: Google. I didn't even get quotes; I got the first one. It didn't tell me which apartment I should get.

All jokes aside, I realize there are fundamental differences in the way health insurance impacts our consumer behavior. But why? I would suggest it's two things: the point of purchasing and the modern-day reliance of the medical community on the network model.

The point of purchasing healthcare is primarily divided into four main categories in the post-ACA world:

- Commercial group insurance, offered by your employer (or the employer of your spouse or parent)
- Individual insurance purchased on or off the exchange
- Public benefits (Medicaid and Medicare)
- Uninsured/cash pay

Now think about how we buy our home and auto insurance, having as many choices as there are colors in a crayon box. You have only two options: insured and uninsured. All purchasing is done by us, the individuals. We either pick a carrier based on price or through an agent we trust to find the best plan. We'll come back to this point of purchasing difference. What about the medical community's dependence on the network model? Here, I'm describing that most healthcare is funneled to providers through PPO networks (or other network arrangements).

In this male-dominated business, where many of my colleagues have been at this longer than I have been alive, I am often immediately discounted as one, someone's assistant or two, a new hire, fresh in the biz. I probably shouldn't admit this in black and white, but I often use this to my advantage. When I first got into the business, I listened in meetings, on calls, at conferences, and on webinars. I've noticed people share more (and juicier) info in the presence of people they think aren't listening, don't get it, or aren't smart enough to do anything with the information. So, there's me—ditzy young'n soaking it all in.

To be fair, we don't get it because we aren't taught *anything* about how it works. We are thrown in. Tools, apps, and companies are available to help consumers navigate the industry. But they are few and far between and even harder to find if you don't know where to look.

Think about what our consumer exposure is to healthcare. We see billboards for insurance carriers, local hospitals, and cancer centers. We watch TV commercials about the best medicine for our condition. Have you ever noticed how there's no mention of price in these commercials? Only if you can't afford your meds, they might be able to help. We'll talk more about this in the next chapter.

We learn about our health from our doctors. We supplement that with what we research on our own. Let's be honest; we all have a Google MD degree. Are you diagnosed with something? Google. Your doctor orders a test? Google. Prescribed something? Google. (But then quickly stop reading because you're not sure if you read all the fine print, you will go through with taking the meds!) It would be interesting to ask doctors how many patients question their treatments now, in the internet age, than they did before.

But I digress. We learn about health from doctors and are told by our health insurance carriers what doctors and hospitals we may go to. We must also ensure that whatever our doctor orders, we can even have it done (unless we want to pay out of pocket).

Considering my earlier example of car insurance, it's not insane for health insurance to control what providers I can visit. If you've ever filed a car insurance claim, you know there are a few steps and sometimes restrictions before you get your repairs. The insurance company may send an adjuster to look at the damage. They may ask you to get repair estimates and give you a network of repair shops they prefer you to use. They may even advise you that if you go to their service provider, you will pay nothing other than your deductible, but if you go to another shop, there's a maximum they will cover.

We accept this process. We may not like it, but we accept it. I do not work in home and auto insurance and can't explain why it works that way. I would guess that the network of service shops has some aggressively priced "deal" with the insurance company based on volume. This makes the insurance company more comfortable using them. We know every claim comes to this process, whether it's hail damage or an accident. It's worth mentioning that often people don't even file claims with their insurance because they don't want to deal with the hassle, restrictions, time, and back and forth. They also don't want their premiums to go up. Now, let's do the same exercise in health insurance.

At the most basic level, we must all realize that every time we engage with the medical system (every ER visit, every checkup, every antibiotic we pick up from the pharmacy), we are essentially filing an insurance claim. Sound familiar? It's worth mentioning that often people don't file claims with their insurance because they don't want to deal with the hassle, restrictions, time, and back and forth. They also don't want their premiums to go up. When we think about it this way, the process is similar; it's just more painful because the frequency of medical insurance claims is dramatically higher than that of our auto insurance claims.

Medical insurance carriers have a network of providers for a reason. If they pay medical claims, they only want to pay them to providers where they have an agreement that works for them. Things have changed a lot since the early formative years of Blue Cross Blue Shield. Insurance companies today are for-profit entities (some publicly held), and their goal is to turn a profit. So, they negotiate contracts with providers they know they can pay and still turn a profit.

On the other side of the negotiation table, you have a provider. For this example, I'm calling a provider any medical provider (doctor, lab, imaging center, hospital, etc.). The provider knows what they need to receive for every medical service they perform. They are also in the business of making a profit— or covering "cost". (There's not enough time to address the non-profit provider here. Note that just because an entity is non-profit does not mean its pricing methodology is charitable).

From the moment you make an appointment, a process is started. It may involve a prior authorization or a verification of benefits and eligibility. It will include a review of your patient responsibility. This is relatively easy if the provider is "in network" with your insurance company. But if they are not, it gets more complicated because they don't have the aforementioned agreement, so what the provider bills and the insurance company pays is more complex.

Then, on the day of your appointment, let's say it's a doctor's visit, your doctor is focused on you, the patient. They are concerned with what labs to order, tests to run, or prescriptions that would be best for you. The doctor rarely is involved in the billing side of the house, and I've discovered that many aren't even sure how it all works. So, they make their orders, and the billing department gets to work. They may have ordered something that isn't covered by your plan. Or, they may have ordered it at a place not in the network. This is where we all get frustrated. But remember, this new test or prescription is like a separate claim (think auto insurance analogy). This process gets significantly worse if a chronic condition is present or long-term treatment protocol is necessary. Many of us have been on the merry-go-round where we ask our doctor's office a question about what we can/can't do, and they advise us to check with our insurance company. We call the insurance company, and they tell us what they recommend, but say we should consult with our doctor. It's because everyone works in a silo. They are focused on their piece of the puzzle. There is little to no cohesion. You, the patient, are left being the leader. And that is the problem; it's like being thrown into a CEO position you're not qualified for, you don't know the people, and you don't even know the work your new company does. Only with medical care can life or death be on the other side of our navigating.

If the US health insurance industry is a scavenger hunt, I have the map. The key to finding where the money is going in US healthcare is misaligned incentives. More on that later.

Hospital, doctor, and health system administrators manage the business side of healthcare. Their incentive is to design contracts and initiatives that keep their doors open, their expenses covered, and hopefully make a profit. Doctors and nurses are focused on meeting their obligations to see patients. Many spend hours charting information simply so they can get paid. Insurance companies are making a profit. Some work to make just enough, and others turn hundreds of billions in profit during a pandemic. Employers are doing their best to offer the best benefits they can afford. Most employers want their employees to be healthy and access the best care but are limited by the egregious insurance costs.

You are trying to stay alive and healthy, but really, you're the CEO of your health and, shockingly, your employees and their family members.

---

1. https://journalofethics.ama-assn.org/article/us-health-care-non-system-1908-2008/2008-05
2. https://www.bcbs.com/articles/health-insurance-invention-innovation-history-of-the-blue-cross-and-blue-shield
    https://advocacy.consumerreports.org/wp-content/uploads/2013/03/yourhealthdollar.org_blue-cross-history-compilation.pdf
3. https://www.bcbs.com/articles/health-insurance-invention-innovation-history-of-the-blue-cross-and-blue-shield
4. https://www.aetna.com/about-us/aetna-history.html
5. https://www.cigna.com/about-us/company-profile/milestones
6. https://finance.yahoo.com/news/unitedhealth-group-history-health-insurance-192731176.html?guce_referrer=aHR0cHM6Ly93d3cuZ29vZ2xlLmNvbvS8&guce_referrer_sig=AQAAAHOVaYUVLOBpHxs9b5WiRyvx-AYkn9HMe5pdWzknP-NiRc2XCb4JH2ge31jZWVLaawcmjx3rut24xi9ZTVSss1wN36Vgb5FDz7ChMO_jvUg27wBYt86sD7xTJ&guccounter=2

CHAPTER 2
THERE'S NO MONEY IN HEALTHY PATIENTS

DR. KRISTINE REGNIER

The healthcare system does not support health promotion; it supports disease management.

———

FOR YEARS, while working within a hospital system, I saw countless employers exhaust extensive resources on wellness programs in hopes of improving their employees' health. Unfortunately, most of them never realized any changes in benefit plan cost or clinical outcomes. Why is this? Let us look at what many vendors in the industry are doing.

THE HOOK

Vendors reach out to employers, touting the importance of instituting a corporate wellness program. Employers are given facts and figures surrounding absenteeism, sick days, and the cost of chronic illness. They are told how a wellness program will improve employee morale, increase productivity, and decrease their benefit spending in the long run. The vendor will recommend screenings to identify what condition(s) the employee population suffers from. Usually, this consists of onsite laboratory and biometric testing such as glucose, a lipid panel or cholesterol, waist circumference, body mass index (BMI), and blood pressure. After the screenings are done, the vendor crunches the numbers and presents you with an aggregate report. It typically shows your employee population is suffering from diabetes or pre-diabetes, hyperlipidemia (high cholesterol), hypertension (high blood pressure), and high body mass index (BMI). You just paid a lot of money to find out essentially useless information. It is no surprise that your population deals with those four issues, the "dreadful four," as I like to call them. Diabetes, hyperlipidemia, hypertension, and obesity are rampant in the U.S. population.

THE PITCH

The vendor will attempt to sell you programs encouraging employees to take better care of themselves. Often these programs are centered on three key areas: weight loss, physical activity, and nutrition education, as if no one realizes that eating well, exercising, and losing weight helps curb the "dreadful four." How often do you hear about the latest weight loss app or see a Peloton ad pop up on your screen?

Many vendors also offer health coaching services to encourage healthy habits. However, the vast majority of health coaches are not medical professionals. Often, they are fitness instructors or personal trainers who take online certification courses, none of which are regulated by state or federal agencies. The complexities of patient issues are too vast and complicated for a fitness instructor or health coach. No offense to those professionals; they do excellent work, but they are not equipped to supplant medical professionals.

To help make the sale, the vendor might present data from other clients claiming that participants in their wellness programs have lower healthcare claims versus those that do not participate. But what about the fact that people who are already physically active and generally healthy, are more likely to participate in wellness programs, so they would naturally have lower claims? The main difficulty with wellness programs is how to account for a significant health event that did not occur. There is no way to show hard dollar savings to prevent someone from having a stroke or heart attack. You would need to jump in the DeLorean time machine with Doc Brown to see how changing a person's habits can alter their future and subsequent medical claims. If only we could.

THE FAILED TOOLS

There are numerous tools to help people lose weight: point counting programs, meal delivery services, local gyms, keto diets, vegan diets, and even bariatric weight loss surgery. Yet, those tools do not seem to work long-term. It's all too common that going to the local gym turns into an unused membership within a few weeks, and diets become too restrictive. Many bariatric surgical patients end up regaining weight within a year or two. The US weight loss market is valued at 58 billion dollars. A study released by Harvard T. H. Chan School of Public Health estimates that about half the US population will be obese by 2030. That is a lot of money spent on an industry that is not producing results. So, where is the disconnect? How can we spend billions of dollars on weight loss as a country only to anticipate that half the population will continue to struggle with obesity? Answer: no one is treating the underlying cause of these health conditions.

FIND THE CAUSE

A person who suffers from one or more of the "dreadful four" knows they need help. Yet, repeatedly, all these tools prove futile because medical professionals fail to look at the entire person: the mental, the emotional, and the physical. Employees are given fragmented, pointed solutions such as an app to track steps, talking to a health coach, logging workouts, and completing screenings, while no one finds the causes of the participants' health issues. Not all wellness programs are a sham; some have benefits, but they are few and far between. The successful programs focus on behavior and lifestyle change and are managed by a medical professional.

Screening seems to be of little benefit because we know a large percentage of our employees will have at least one of the "dreadful four" based on the current health of the US population. The fragmented tools currently offered do not seem to produce lasting benefits. To whom do we turn to help our employees uncover the underlying cause of their illnesses? Answer: Primary Care (when done well and effectively).

THE PITFALLS OF PRIMARY CARE

Many of us have had similar experiences when visiting our primary care providers, who perform a quick once-over exam. Your doctor will have a medical assistant take your weight, temperature, and blood pressure. The doctor will listen to your heart and lungs, make recommendations, and you are out the door. Often, patients feel they did not have their concerns thoroughly addressed and, most importantly, listened to. Why? Answer: the healthcare system does not support health promotion; it supports disease management.

DISEASE MANAGEMENT

Major healthcare systems employ teams of nurses who provide care management. The nurses are tasked with utilizing data and internal referrals, seeking high-cost claimants and those with complex health conditions. They form relationships with patients and support them throughout their journeys. These nurses work diligently to help patients manage their health condition(s). To be clear, the nurses working in care management are doing extraordinary work. I have seen the impact care navigation can have on a person's life, and I applaud our nurses. However, what is being done to prevent a person from having multiple diagnoses, an overflowing medicine cabinet, trips to numerous specialists, and the need for care navigation in the first place? Answer: nothing, because there is no money made with healthy patients.

HEALTHY PATIENTS DO NOT PRODUCE REVENUE

In the not-too-distant past, hospitals functioned to provide urgent care during life-threatening events. But the business model of healthcare systems has changed. If you look around your community, you will likely see that the majority of ancillary centers are owned by healthcare systems, such as immediate care facilities, imaging centers, and cancer treatment facilities, to name a few. When looking for a primary care provider or specialist, your options are mostly physicians employed by the healthcare system. The reason for this is to increase revenue. Healthcare systems are buying up physician practices by the dozens in order to direct downstream revenue. Employed physicians are expected to make referrals to facilities within the healthcare system that employs them. To explain how this works, let us look at an example: Rosie is a fifty-year-old woman with diabetes, is morbidly obese, and has been having a lot of knee pain.

She goes to her primary care provider, employed by the local healthcare system, to address her knee pain. The doctor recommends imaging and refers her to the healthcare system's imaging center. It is diagnosed that she will need her knee replaced. Her doctor then refers her to an orthopedic surgeon, again employed by the healthcare system. The surgeon repairs her knee and refers her to physical therapy, again, a part of the healthcare system. Rosie slowly recovers and realizes that if she was not severely overweight, she might not have had a knee issue. She decides to go back to her primary care doctor to discuss options. The doctor refers her to their bariatric department for a consultation. Rosie meets with a physician who recommends that she undergo weight loss surgery. Rosie follows the recommendation and has the surgery. The hospital system has captured revenue from primary care provider visits, imaging, orthopedic surgery, physical therapy, and bariatric surgery. What would have been two $100 visits has now turned into thousands of dollars in revenue for the healthcare system from Rosie's care. Most healthcare reimbursement is a fee-for-service model, which allows healthcare systems to collect more while the employer's health plan is footing the bill.

VALUE-BASED CARE (VBC) - IS CHANGE ON THE HORIZON?

There has been much buzz around VBC models in recent years. These new models for providing healthcare aim to increase quality and cut costs. On the surface, these programs seem to have benefits, rewarding providers based on the outcomes of their patient population. But looking deeper into how these contracts operate, we are left with the question: what is being done to treat the underlying cause of disease?

VBC contracts come in many forms and can be complex regarding the reimbursement structure. Here we will look at it with a simplified example. VBC contracts are an agreement between a provider organization or healthcare system and, usually, an insurance carrier or, in the case of Centers for Medicare and Medicaid Services, the federal government. These contracts stipulate specific goals providers need to meet regarding patient outcomes, such as the percentage of generic medications prescribed, percentage of patients with Hemoglobin A1c at the optimal level, emergency department utilization, patient experience ratings, and so on. Combined, these various goals are termed quality metrics. Depending upon the provider group's performance on these metrics, they can be rewarded financially.

One standard quality metric is Statin therapy for the prevention and treatment of cardiovascular disease. This metric rewards providers who prescribe statin medications to lower a patient's cholesterol. Utilizing cholesterol-lowering medications is a standard of care, and there is no arguing that these medications should be used when appropriate. But what is often lacking is the next step: What is the *cause* of the patient's high cholesterol? Is it their diet, lack of exercise, are they smokers, or are they overweight? Is the physician doing anything to address these underlying causes? Under VBC contracts, providers are not rewarded for taking the time to uncover the actual cause of a patient's condition. Instead, they are given a list of boxes to check at each patient visit. But isn't it important to reward providers for working with patients on lifestyle modifications to eventually remove the need for their medication? The same can be said for other metrics related to diabetes, one of which is performing a yearly retinal exam. Again, clinically appropriate and needed for diabetic patients, but where is the reward for transforming a patient's health status and not simply managing their disease?

PRIMARY CARE DOES NOT PROMOTE HEALTH

We should not blame physicians for the shortcomings we see in primary care today. The fact is that the healthcare system is to blame. Primary care providers are expected to refer in-house so that healthcare systems can beef up the bottom line, are hamstrung by the demands of insurance contracts, and have an overwhelming patient load due to the shortage of physicians going into primary care. Primary care providers are burnt out and do not have the bandwidth to promote health. Something must change.

SOLUTION

Seek to utilize independent primary care providers. An independent physician does not have allegiance to a particular healthcare system and is more objective in their referral process and treatment. As a small business owner, the independent primary care provider has more skin in the game. They will focus on the quality of care they provide, knowing their patients are the best referral source.

Direct primary care (DPC) is an emerging model transforming how health care is delivered and paid for. In the DPC model, a physician charges a monthly membership fee that includes office visits, various procedures, and testing. DPC models also cap the number of patients accepted into the practice. This allows the doctor to have longer visits with patients, usually around 45 minutes (have you spent 45 minutes with your doctor?), a manageable number of patients, and the ability to focus solely on the practice of medicine. Looking back at our example of Rosie, if her physician could spend more time with her, perhaps the underlying cause of her obesity could have been treated. She would likely have been in a much better state of health.

This model, with a limited number of patients, increased time for office visits, services in one place managed by a medical professional, and no competing incentives, has the power to transform primary care.

It would also eliminate the failed corporate wellness programs we see today. The doctors in this model have the time to focus on their patients, uncover the cause of illness, and collaborate with their patients, moving from disease management and putting the health back into healthcare.

CHAPTER 3
THANK YOU, DR. P.

DR. MADELINE SMITH

Health insurance doesn't save lives.

———

IF I HEAR one more person tell me that "healthcare is broken," I might audibly scream. And not a cute dainty scream, but an ear-piercing, "I can't take it anymore. What the fuck is wrong with you?" scream. Not the scream that suits this professional lady in business. It is not that I disagree with the statement. But to say healthcare is broken is about as descriptive or helpful as saying becoming a parent is different from having a parent. To say healthcare is broken implies that it was once together and whole but no longer is, and perhaps a certain someone broke it.

Talking about the broken healthcare system was a progressive sales pitch ten years ago. It was as if you were a fearless warrior brave enough to acknowledge out loud that there were deficiencies; you were a pioneer. Maybe on the heels of the Affordable Care Act, everyday people started to think about healthcare differently.

As an employer, you probably know the issues we battle in healthcare and insurance. We all are working toward the same goal, or at least we say we are and should be.

Usually, what we hear about healthcare being broken is about the insurance/payor side of the house being a deficient, convoluted, often corrupt space. Employers, employees, and their dependent family members do not and could not be expected to understand the complexity of what is behind the curtain. They trust many of us to guide them. We can only do that if we are not part of the problem ourselves.

I think of it like internet service. Wi-Fi in our homes is this magical, wonderful tool we have become obsessively dependent on. This becomes painfully obvious when we find ourselves without it. I must confess that I am perhaps the least technically inclined/mechanical human you've met. It's no surprise to many modern-day parents that my kids can teach me a thing or two about technology. It's not impressive that my grandpa probably could connect something via Bluetooth faster than I could. Let's just say I have many gifts; technical savvy is not one of them.

I expect my Wi-Fi to work like magic. When we moved into our new house, I knew the most critical service appointment I had to make was our internet service. Aren't they magical? They are the gatekeepers to the world of unhealthy movie binging, overworking, and time-wasting; we rely heavily on them. So, I scheduled the appointment so the technician would beat us to the house, and we would have Wi-Fi before our first box was unpacked. I didn't want to spend minutes without service. Or, more accurately, I must confess, I didn't want my kids and their tablets without Wi-Fi while we were unpacking.

The technician showed up, plugged things in, and put wires in places that seemed counterintuitive. He wrote the secret passcode on a card and left. We called him back a few days later when something wasn't working. Nothing I heard him say to my husband made sense. It was like hearing someone speak Mandarin. And frankly, I didn't care. Just. Make. It. Work. And thankfully, he did. I acknowledge the first-world problems and privilege here for what it's worth.

I think that's what healthcare and the insurance mechanism are for most people. They don't understand it, and frankly, they don't want to. It's our job to make it work. Now more than ever, the expectation is that we make it work, make it cheaper, and improve the experience. Trust me when I say if there was a way we could fix it, there are many of us who would. I hate to break it to you, but there's also another faction. Their goal is to pretend to fix it. All while making bank.

Before getting into the healthcare/insurance industry, I was clueless. That's probably an understatement of my extreme lack of knowledge. I not only knew nothing, but like many of us, I was utterly confident that I knew enough. I had been on my mother's health plan until I got my first job with health benefits. Emancipating myself from her plan was an impressive sign of independence (and one less thing she could hold over my head).

As a young adult, I was lucky if I remembered to get an annual exam. That honestly only happened if my physician had a robust enough system to send automated reminders. I was blessed not to have any chronic conditions and never needed to familiarize myself personally with how it all worked. Plus, I knew I had a plastic credit card thingy in my wallet that took care of everything.

I'll never forget this call I had with the financial department of the local hospital where I delivered my oldest son. Remembering it even now makes a prickly heat rise through my face. As I remember, I want to crawl under my desk with embarrassment. I wish I knew whom I talked to twelve years ago so I could call them and apologize for being such an ignorant asshole (not much of which I could blame on postpartum hormones). I got a bill that said I owed more money than I could understand. So, I called the 800 number on the paper and pressed buttons until I got a human. Then I explained, "I got this paper in the mail, and it says I owe a lot of money, and I don't. I have insurance."

After she got my information and looked me up in her system, she calmly explained that I was looking at an explanation of benefits. I vividly remember getting kind of bitchy with her and saying something to the effect of, "This doesn't look like a benefit to me." She explained that this tells me what my insurance covered and what I may still owe.

This is where it gets embarrassing...

"But I have insurance, and this was all supposed to be covered."

I knew nothing. And how was I supposed to? Who would explain it? The HR employee who had helped me sign up for the benefits at the non-profit I worked at? She barely understood it. I asked her a question about the two plans, and she said, "All I know is this one has less that comes out of your check each week," so that's the one I picked.

Girl, if I could find you now.

Many might say, "What about my Summary of Benefits?" What is that? Some paper in a new hire folder? We are more concerned with our pay, hours, and lunch schedule than how our health plan works when we first enter the workforce.

I wasn't an idiot because healthcare's broken. I was uninformed because no one taught me how to navigate healthcare. I've since learned that the system is intentionally complex and aims to serve businesses and people who are, well, not you, me, or our employees.

So how *do* we learn to navigate it? For many of us, it is an expensive trial and error. Some nice person working in billing at a doctor's office takes five extra minutes out of their day to explain one piece to you. Or you discover the hard way what deductibles and copays are and how there are millions of exceptions to the concepts you think you've figured out.

If you pay attention, you quickly learn that the insurance card does little. It's not much different from your Costco/Sam's card. You pay for it; it gets you access, but you better be willing to bring the real dough when you shop.

As a kid, my family didn't have cable, so I was stuck watching whatever was on the four local stations on the nineteen-inch TV we shared in the family room. When I was home sick from school, my mom would make me a grilled cheese with tomatoes and let me watch *ER* and *Law & Order* (we laugh about this now as it was probably not the most appropriate kid-friendly TV). To this day, they are my comfort food and shows. For some strange reason, my three boys don't share this appreciation.

I remember watching *ER* and thinking about how fascinating it was. Being a doctor seemed like so much fun. They work for a while and then spend most of their time in the breakroom or living these fantasy lives. Then in high school, *Grey's Anatomy* debuted. This, at least, highlighted the heart-wrenching side of the work. Everyone was still gorgeous, and breakrooms (or supply closets) were the scene setting for at least 50 percent of each episode, but they talked about real things. Things like treatment not being approved by insurance and families not being able to afford care.

Then the movie *John Q.* was devastating and raw. We all absorbed that movie as if it was just another blockbuster. Plus, who doesn't love a good Denzel flick? But did we learn anything? Doubtful. Many didn't pick up on the not-so-subtle commentary about the managed care world and some of the ugliness.

What about the even older scenes of healthcare? The ones you click through on AMC or Turner Classic Movies when you are channel surfing. The ones tucked away in classics we reinvigorate once a year on holidays like *It's a Wonderful Life.* Doctors in the towns knew your whole family. In the Westerns, they used a good whiskey for anesthetic, antiseptic, or both. We are transported into those old movies and see the pharmacy had the best malts in those tall, authentic shake glasses, not just the prescriptions they compounded by hand. They knew everyone in town, everyone's kids, and all the gossip. Even if it was an idyllic made-for-TV version, that was more like what healthcare was back then. Much of it happened in your own home.

Today, we have a risk-based financial exchange system where people's "alive-ness" is monitored, observed, and occasionally affected. That's what we are caring for and referring to 80 percent of the time: life—keeping patients alive. Anything more is on the fringe. Yes, entire healthcare divisions are devoted to pain management, mental health, and substance abuse treatment. Still, they are marginalized and often stigmatized by the system they are a part of, the payment methodology they must all depend on, and even society.

I'm sure our familiarity with this is like the six degrees of Kevin Bacon or the anecdote you are never over six feet from a spider. We've all either experienced or know someone who's had a test of their aliveness within the flawed system we have today. Sometimes, it's relatively uneventful, but other times it is either a marvelous success or a devastating failure.

Mine was a dramatic display of the system at work and, thankfully, at a time when I was finally knowledgeable enough to navigate its Alice in Wonderland-like complexity. I had worked in insurance for a few years, understood that my magic plastic card was nothing more than an access pass, and knew what questions to ask. I was early post-partum, having had my youngest son a week prior. My husband and I could count our total combined hours of sleep on one hand. We were in that exhausted place all new parents know, where you're lucky to eat, shower, and nap all in one day.

With two older boys (two and seven years old) needing us, we were deep into the parenting twilight zone. I vividly remember sitting down in the playroom with the baby to change his diaper while my husband was doing something with the other boys in the kitchen. I needed more wipes and called out to him. When he came to me with the wipes, I talked, or at least sounds came out of my mouth. None made sense as he looked at me, perplexed. Now I was annoyed.

Why isn't he answering me?

"Are you being funny right now?" he asked, unsure if I was being silly or trying to start an argument (not that I would do such a thing on a typical day).

More nonsense came out of my mouth, and I realized the right side of my face was slowly cooperating less and less. I felt it dripping down and not keeping up with the left side. Then my right hand went numb and cold. I couldn't feel the wipes anymore. This feeling crept up my right arm. Everything was happening fast and painfully slow at the same time.

What happened next is a blur. Looking back, we handled it terribly. The hospital was less than a mile down the street. My mom was less than five minutes away at work, so I think he called her, or maybe I did, but in some mysterious way, she appeared at the house and took me to the ER. The incapacitating session had only lasted a few minutes, and I was back to normal but was already headed to the ER by then. I vaguely remember my husband saying he was calling 911, but I brushed it off. The time it would take them and the bill we would get dictated my decision to have her take me to the hospital.

When we got to the ER, she signed us in, and we waited. It had that sterile ER smell and crisp coolness to prevent germs from taking over.

The waiting room was solemn and almost silent, although full of people, except for *Judge Judy* on the tiny TV in the corner. We waited for an eternity, and then they called me back. After a battery of tests, I lay on the exam table while a resident and neurologist debated what they thought was the cause. Maybe it was supposed to be a bed, but it was hard metal and felt like what I imagined the tables at the morgues feel like. The resident thought it was a TIA, which she told me was like a mini-stroke. The neurologist said she was sure it was an ocular migraine. I didn't know what either was. I knew I should be at home with my babies.

My face is working; get me off this table.

I looked at my mom and raised an eyebrow as the two argued over me. Eventually, the neurologist won in the most dismissive way possible to the resident. The resident gave up, embarrassed. The neurologist was comforting and so sure of herself as she told me they would get me out of there quickly. They sent me home with discharge papers that said little of anything, with a reminder in bold to come back if the symptoms reoccurred.

If only I could tell them what happened next. If only I could find that resident and tell her to trust herself and her instincts and not let her age create a deafening doubt within herself throughout her career. I tell myself it didn't, and she's somewhere saving lives and likely doing the same thing to her residents now.

Fast forward a few weeks; my newborn wouldn't sleep in his bassinet unless I was on the floor next to him. So, like any parent who has mastered the art of concession out of necessity, my husband bought a twin-size mattress for me to put on the floor next to him. I slept there like an eleven-year-old at church camp for the next several months. I woke up morning after morning with back and chest pain that I could only relieve with ibuprofen or rounding my back like I was doing the Cat-Cow yoga position.

Eventually, the pain worsened, and my breath became labored at times. I finally went to urgent care (knowing this was a more cost-conscious option than the ER). The physician I saw said he thought it was a Pulmonary Embolism and I needed to go to the ER. He wanted to call an ambulance, but I refused. My husband was outside in the car with the kids, so I said he would take me, much to the physician's dissatisfaction. They called ahead to warn them I was coming and what he suspected the issue was. After signing in and waiting for an hour and a half, they took me back for an EKG. Knowing what I know about pulmonary embolisms, it seems odd that this was all they did.

Isn't an EKG for your heart?

But what do I know?

I'm not a doctor.

To them, I looked fine. I was twenty-nine-years-old, appeared healthy, had no chronic or genetic conditions, no history of anything really, and aside from some chest pain, my aliveness got an A+ grade.

After the EKG was normal, the physician said it was probably a pinched nerve. I could stay and have them run more tests, but it would likely be another few hours. I remember thinking, *obviously, I'm not dying. It's not a pulmonary embolism, or they wouldn't send me to a room to wait a few more hours.*

I signed the discharge papers against medical advice and left. I don't blame them. Truly. I'm the one who signed the document. If they gave me the same information, I would still do the same thing if I could go back and do it again. I had no idea I would knock on death's door in no time. I thought my aliveness score was solid.

Plus, it's probably because I'm sleeping on this damn cheap mattress.

Or maybe it's because I'm so out of shape.

I'll work out and make healthier choices, returning to a regular adult bed; maybe that will all help.

Over the next few weeks, I made those changes. I despised running more than dental work. But I trained for and ran my first 5k, all while popping Ibuprofen like a daily multivitamin. I was functioning. I was alive. My maternity leave ended, and I returned to work. A few months later, we relocated to another state. A couple of weeks later, the daily pain was overpowering the Ibuprofen's impact. I had a day of meetings downtown. Looking back, it must have been the adrenaline of my boss being in town and my obligation to present in front of numerous clients, meeting after meeting, that kept me going.

I texted my husband during my last meeting and told him I needed him to pick me up; I couldn't physically drive home. The pain was too

THANK YOU, DR. P.   29

bad, and now my breathing was becoming difficult. He took me to the ER nearest our home so he was close with the boys if I needed him.

The attending physician looked at me and said he was sure it was my gallbladder. It seemed like a strange guess, but again, I'm no doctor. I sat in the flimsy gown, trying to work from my phone while they drew blood and took me down the hall for a scan. Time passed, and it turned out my gallbladder was in great shape, but there was a blood test that looked odd, so they did a CT scan. Looking back, the doctor was cryptic. I now understand why. I didn't know then how worried I should be.

As long as I can keep working, I'm fine.

They will not let me die at Urgent Care, so I'm going with the flow.

I got back to the room, it was freezing, and the remote wasn't working, so I was stuck watching the Weather Channel. My phone stopped blowing up with work calls and emails, and texts, so there was no more work I could do to distract me. The attending physician has since become a known figure in my family to this day. We lovingly call him Dr. P., not because we've ever dealt with him again after this incident, but because his name tag is branded into my mind because he's the one who saved my life.

Dr. P. eventually came to the room and pulled back the curtain. He had two gentlemen with him whom I hadn't seen before. They weren't dressed like nurses or techs or doctors. Dr. P. approached the right side of my bed and placed his hand on my shin over the blanket I was burying myself under because I was so cold. I was half-listening to him and half-monitoring these guys coming up to the left side of my bed. I noticed the doctor's face was white. Ghost white. If I didn't know better, I would've thought he was trying not to cry.

He talked in a quiet, almost patronizing voice. "So, while I'm talking to you, these guys are with the ambulance, and they will strap you to your bed while I talk. It turns out that the blood test was right; you have a blood clot. In fact, both of your lungs are full of blood clots."

He was talking faster than I could keep up, and my eyes filled with tears.

"Unfortunately, the hospital here doesn't have what they need to care for you, so we've called the main hospital in Dallas, and they are expecting you. You should call whomever you need to and let them know where you are headed and that they should hurry to meet you there."

As he was talking, my legs and chest were being strapped gently but securely to the bed, and my bed was being placed onto the gurney. As I was wheeled down the hall and out to the ambulance, Dr. P. shook my hand and said, "I'm so sorry you're going through this. Good luck."

The resident was right. The Urgent Care doc was right. As I would discover later, I had been living with not just one pulmonary embolism but upwards of thirty in each lung for approximately six months thanks to a postpartum deep vein thrombosis that broke into tiny clots.

All I could think about was my sons, my husband, and then ...

How much is this ambulance ride going to cost?

Damn it, I will probably have to stay the night.

He's going to have all the boys by himself.

I'm going to be at this hospital alone.

What will happen with my meetings tomorrow?

Shit, I can't afford a hospital stay.

Am I going to die?

After more than two weeks in the ICU, I quickly learned that the logistics were the least of my worries. Angels in scrubs and hourly blood draws monitoring the effectiveness of my new best friend, a blood thinner, saved my life.

I try to be easy on my earlier self. I acted with the information I had. I had to make choices about my care based on three factors: one, the price of healthcare; two, the expert opinions; and three, my perception (and theirs) of my alive-ness.

The system is not just broken or commercialized. It's a clusterfuck. It's been taken over by capitalistic interests, which could work efficiently if people understood who all the players were and the rules. We, as consumers, must regain our power in navigating the system. Industry professionals must be honest about what's happening and battle the misaligned incentives that have perverted the system from the inside out.

There are no more town doctors making house calls (or are there?). Health insurance doesn't save lives. We are drowning the lifesavers with the thousands of clicks they must chart at night after a day of getting patients in, treated, and out every fifteen minutes. Medical school doesn't train physicians on how to run healthcare businesses and forgets to mention that most of their day, they will deal with commercial payer obligations they must fulfill to get paid 180 days later.

But doctors are all millionaires, right? Who are they to complain about doing their jobs?

Look at how expensive healthcare is - it's all their fault.

Or is it?

CHAPTER 4
THEY ARE NOT THE ENEMY

BLAKE ALLISON

The need to align the clinical strategy with the accountable provider network is essential.

———

ONE OF THE most common misconceptions throughout the healthcare benefit space is that the entire universe would be better if the providers would lower their prices for all their services, stop marketing their services and technology, and essentially become a "price-taker." While the price of a healthcare service is undoubtedly a driver, it must be appropriately combined with the issues driving the employer's health insurance costs. To put this in the simplest terms, let's examine Medicare. Medicare is the federal health insurance program with the best pricing in the world. Yet each year, the headline is how the program goes bankrupt as overall cost spirals out of control. How can this be? Any health plan paying providers 100 percent of Medicare would be the lowest-cost health plan in the country. Yet, everyone is pushing Medicare Advantage (a private health plan offering Medicare benefits) and risk-based models to attempt to curb the cost. The reason for this is that we must have an honest discussion about what drives the per beneficiary per year cost, and I would like to "unpack" these in an attempt to provide some additional clarity. The first is to outline two critical equations clearly:

$$\frac{\text{Total Cost of Care}}{\textit{Price of the Unit of Service x Total Number of Units}} = \textit{Per Beneficiary}$$
$$\textit{Per Year (PBPY) Cost}$$
$$\frac{\text{Total Employer Cost}}{\textit{PBPY + Administrative Costs}} = \textit{Total Employer Cost}$$

I've outlined these equations to examine the myriad forces in addition to the unit of service price that drives your total employer cost. The goal is to simultaneously attack each of these drivers to take control of your healthcare costs.

COST DRIVERS:

Price of the unit of service: Let's start with the elephant in the room, which is the price of a unit of service at a healthcare provider (supplier of all healthcare services). This is part of the overall equation and something that must be addressed. The reality is that the utilization of both the payors and reference-based pricing (RBP) solutions have had a counter effect on getting reasonable prices. The overarching reason is that neither model has created value for the supplier (the healthcare provider). I could write an entire article on the reasons for the prices we have today, but I will skip over some traditional ones and focus on two core concepts:

Market share growth: This is where the two popular models, BUCAH —an acronym for "Blue Cross, United, Cigna, Aetna, and Humana," (often used to describe large carrier-owned fully insured plans) and RBP (referenced-based pricing) have created issues. Most healthcare systems are in a competitive environment, and they have little control due to how a health system gains market share. The unplanned nature of healthcare and economic misalignments leaves them with few levers to grow market share. The first response was to integrate to capture scale and service delivery horizontally and vertically across the broadest care continuum possible. An example is the acquisition of ambulatory surgery centers as care transitioned to the outpatient setting.

Additionally, the initial entrance of managed care created the concept of discounts to participate in preferred networks (remember, a PPO is called a Preferred Provider Organization) designed to drive growth. Still, every plan quickly included every provider, which removed the discount for steerage opportunities. As more employers embraced the model, the health systems were left with only one solution: increasing prices to compensate for the lack of steerage through the PPO mechanism. This is where RBP quickly became an issue: they went after price with no built-in steerage, thus diluting any advantage to the health system (which we must remember is the entity that delivers needed care). High utilization of BUCAH and RBP accelerates this process and is the cause for the recent issues both from a pricing and disruption perspective.

Market advantage: I typically hear this argument about the lack of a marketplace and price transparency when I attend conferences. While that is somewhat true, there is a tendency to ignore the other elements of a free market in that a higher-quality supplier can create a market advantage. For example, suppose every health system is in a PPO and paid essentially the same. In that case, I neither understand how it is "preferred," nor do I understand how a high-quality provider (defined with national metrics) cannot drive a higher price. Anyone who attempts to be competitive on price or quality in the BUCAH or RBP world cannot create differentiation. Given the focus on cost, any new entrant with a lower price creates a market loss. Due to the lack of the ability to drive pricing differentiation based upon service delivery, the focus is exclusively on pricing to counter the lack of market advantage. Various centers of excellence accelerated this. Local providers who weren't willing to discount a high-quality service lost market advantage to entities from other markets who undercut them on price. If a local provider has the best-in-class transplant program, why do employers carve it out? Because of this: they must focus on the price to be paid as much as possible because they cannot drive their market advantage.

Total Number of Units: While we have addressed the issue of price and how it impacts the total cost, the accelerant of that issue is the total number of units or overall utilization of healthcare services by the members on the plan. The ongoing challenge for the employer is that they have a spectrum with some members utilizing meager amounts of healthcare (20-40 percent may not have a claim in a given year) to those with medical conditions driving high utilization levels. Until recently, the providers did not have the structure, resources, or focus on extending clinical care beyond the primary care office to engage members before the need for care. The Affordable Care Act created the catalyst for clinical delivery transformation and for providers to consider the total cost of care. This aligned them with employers for the first time, developing clinical delivery systems to manage this metric. While this was initially very positive, there once again were barriers to rapid adoption:

Expertise: Given the newness of this activity, there were certainly growing pains with the providers. That said, since 2013, many have moved through that and even come to a place of being accredited by national care management entities (NCQA and URAC).

Competition: In the absence of the providers being engaged, third-party payors and stand-alone companies began to sell medical management to employers to drive down the total number of units and curb utilization. As the providers entered the space, the gaps in the third-party models were quickly understood. Still, payors and others used their leverage to maintain the revenue stream (connecting the use of a TPA or network for the requirement to use a specific medical management system).

To further complicate the issue of medical management and utilization, the use of broad networks allowed members to move freely across a vast network of providers, driving higher fragmentation and the risk of multiple services being delivered. The need to align the clinical strategy with the accountable provider network is essential. The most significant challenge with the Medicare Shared Savings Program is that the federal government cannot set up benefit designs that align the member's primary care physician with the downstream care continuum. This, among other drivers, was the catalyst for the adoption of Medicare Advantage plans which were able to create more tightly aligned provider networks. While it will be perceived as a limited choice, the counter is a reduction of fragmentation as a member navigates the healthcare system in alignment with their physician.

Administrative Costs: The last driver of the overall cost to the employer are the administrative costs associated with providing benefits to the employees and their dependents. While some of these are inherently known, these have little to do with the delivery of clinical services, remain outside of the purview of the providers, and generally go towards "rent seekers" who do little to add value to the buyer and supplier relationship. These come in many shapes and forms:

- claims administration costs
- medical management
- utilization management
- complex case management
- concierge programs
- pharmacy
- network access fees
- broker commissions
- general administrative overhead (embedded with all partners, but specifically a driver of increase for the traditional payors)
- Other – anything that any entity would like to charge

SOLUTIONS

Network strategy: As we discussed the drivers of the price per unit of service, we must consider the counter to that issue by aligning the interests of all parties. The pricing issue will follow if the buyer (employer) is willing to align with a particular health system (supplier). The ability to "discount" for added value is a fundamental element that can be achieved. This does require choices regarding providers, which can be disruptive. Still, as the members move from their physicians (there are solutions to keep members aligned with their physicians) into the more costly settings, the employer can use the network strategy to lower the price per unit. That said, the network should be completely adequate, have every specialty (just not every specialist), and be aligned with a high-quality provider focused on value-based care.

Provider-led care management: Once the network has been determined, the key is to wrap as many clinical programs as possible around the providers participating in the network. To the previous point, the more clinical programs can align with the overall provider network, keeping both healthcare as close to the member and the providers as possible, coupled with alignment around service delivery, better quality, and lower utilization, lower cost can be achieved. Additionally, the engagement rate of the members who need to be in a medical management program increases when they understand that the medical management component is integrated with their provider.

Administrative costs: This area doesn't specifically change during the year, but several hidden costs need to be exposed. The first element is PEPM (per employee per month) versus variable pricing. I would challenge any structure, not built on a PEPM, with a clear focus on delivering value and dependence upon a renewal versus creating misaligned incentives that manifest themselves in the claims. A simple example is any type of network fee that depends upon a percentage of the savings. If there is a higher yield to discount from a higher starting point, how is the employer sure they are always getting the same price?

Simply put, if I can contract for a service at $1,000, billed at $5,000, and get paid a PEPM to access that service as many times as needed, and the $4,000 savings is applied to the employer, that is ideal. In a percent of savings scenario, I would be incentivized to find the $6,000 billed event and negotiate down to $1,500. On paper, it seems to be a $4,500 savings from the billed, but the plan paid more for the unit of service. Also, there needs to be a clear understanding of all fees paid by all parties associated with the plan. What fees are being paid to the broker from any of the vendors? What fees are the vendors being paid by the other vendors? Effectively, is everyone working in the best interest of the employer? Transparency is a trendy word and should be applied equally across the entire benefit plan.

The general sentiment across much of the employee health benefit landscape is that the price of the unit of service with a healthcare provider is the primary driver of costs in the United States. While price is always an issue, this has come from the fact that the provider is not typically directly involved with the employee health benefit strategy and deployment; instead, these conversations are held by the employer with other third parties who are working to protect their revenue stream while focusing the issue on the party who is not represented. As you go into the next strategy meeting, please consider the following questions:

1. Am I paying for providers that are not being utilized?
2. Do I have the best possible deal with the local healthcare provider?
3. Is the medical management strategy positioned to maximize engagement, align members with their providers, and focused on the entire care continuum?
4. Who is getting paid? Who pays them? How much are they being paid in deploying my employee health benefits strategy?

These questions will help to draw out near-term opportunities to drive lower cost, higher quality, and better service, which translate to better healthcare value.

$$V_{(VALUE)} = \frac{Q_{(QUALITY)} + S_{(SERVICE)}}{\$_{(COST)}}$$

CHAPTER 5
THIS ISN'T WALL STREET: TREND IS NOT YOUR FRIEND

HILARY GERAGHTY

Change can be disruptive, but it is manageable.

———

INVESTORS WITH 401(K)S, Individual Retirement Accounts (IRAs), and other retail investment accounts understand the value of investing for the long term. Instead of trying to time the market, investors employ a dollar cost averaging method. Dollar-cost averaging is a simple, cost-effective way of saving for retirement while leveraging the power of compounded returns to accumulate wealth. On Wall Street, it is said that "Trend is your friend!" meaning if the investor knows the general multi-year direction of the market, it will allow them to tweak their portfolio to improve performance and reduce risk. The trend of the market is ubiquitous; it is discussed daily on *Bloomberg TV, MSNBC,* and many other reputable news channels. The Federal Reserve and most politicians in America routinely offer analysis on the state of the economy as either growing or shrinking. An investor would need to unplug themselves from all news and social media outlets not to detect the market trend. It makes one ask:

- Why is there so much noise about market trend on Wall Street but relatively little noise on healthcare trend?
- Why do investors talk about compounded returns in the stock market and not compounded returns (losses) on their healthcare plans?
- Why do companies spend substantial energy managing the assets on their balance sheets (investment returns) but much less on their liabilities (healthcare plans and underlying cost drivers)?

HIDDEN IN PLAIN SITE

Year after year, large, fully insured carriers and administrative services only (ASO) providers (more on this later) fully disclose their annual "unsustainable" plan cost increases (trend). Most insurance producers keep marketing and selling their plans, and most employer groups keep buying it. It is a vicious cycle with no end in sight. Are profits increasing 8-12 percent year after year? Are employee wages increasing this amount?

WHAT IS HEALTHCARE TREND?

Healthcare trend is not based on a group's claims experience. Simply put, trend reflects the percent change in the cost and the utilization of healthcare services in our economy. Let's illustrate with a real-life example. When a hospital system buys out an independent physician practice, two things happen that have a direct impact on medical trends:

A Cost Driver: As a new facility in the hospital system, the physician's practice now bills their services as a hospital outpatient provider. This subtle change, which most patients do not realize, will significantly impact cost. Let's focus on cancer treatments for a moment and look at one actuarial study that measured the cost differences of several common chemotherapy treatments in a hospital outpatient setting (HOP) versus a provider's office (POV).[1] Once the researchers normalized the data to illustrate a true "apples to apples" comparison, they noted the HOP costs were 28-53 percent higher than the POV. The only difference was the "site" of care. This illustrates a good example of the cost component of trend.

A Utilization Driver: In 1992, the US Government passed the 340B Drug Pricing Program, which requires drug manufacturers to provide outpatient care drugs to eligible healthcare and other organizations like Medicaid and other covered entities at drastically reduced prices.

It was supposed to help the poor, but thirty years later, the 340B has morphed into a huge profit center for those qualified facilities. They can buy prescription drugs for half price while still billing patients with insurance for the full price of the medication. This program abuse has been a windfall for the hospital systems and a driving force behind the consolidations in healthcare, such as the buying out of physician practices, from primary care providers to oncologists. Medscape, a global leader in online medical news and research, reports that hospital systems now employ over 71 percent of oncologists.[2] What is most interesting about the report is that most providers become employees because they want a more conventional schedule, reliable income, and less time focusing on running a business. This offers an obvious appeal for many physicians, but the downside for patients and payors is that hospital administrators and stakeholders now seize control over the providers. They know what services offer the highest margins and build the provider's compensation plans around those models.

Many physicians get into medicine because they feel the calling to help others. It is a very noble profession, a position of trust for the public. But for the physician's office owned by a large hospital system, the cost of drugs and services administered in their office will be marked up an average of 30-50 percent. The increased utilization due to their new employer's profit-driven policies and procedures is but "one" driver of this unsustainable trend.

A ZERO SUM GAME

National spending on healthcare in the U.S. exceeds four trillion dollars a year and is quickly approaching 20 percent of the gross domestic product (GDP). It is big business with years of low-interest record rates (cheap money) and lax anti-trust regulatory oversight. The large, fully insured carriers and hospital systems have rapidly grown through horizontal and vertical integrations. Everyone is in everyone else's lane these days, and it can be difficult to identify many hidden conflicts of interest.

Most people agree that there is a great deal of waste in the system. The Journal of the American Medical Association (JAMA) Network finds the estimated waste in healthcare to be around 25 percent.[3] However, many industry insiders estimate this number to be closer to 30 to 40 percent. Regardless of which estimate is used, it is still a significant number, and all plan sponsors should be focused on reducing this wasteful spending.

The critical factor employers need to understand is a 25-40 percent reduction in plan cost is a 25-40 percent reduction in revenues for interested parties. Naturally, these other parties will fight to preserve their revenues and resist changing the status quo. For them, the system is working fine!

For a plan sponsor that is considering implementing a value-based model, disruption is inevitable, and the program will naturally face several headwinds. Healthcare is complicated, and when considering options, it would be prudent to acknowledge the "obvious" conflicts of interest of the different parties that have a financial stake in the conversation:

The Hospital Administrators: It is said that hospital administrators are the most trusted members of the communities, yet they are the most hesitant to embrace transparency. Their resolve to maintain the status quo and obfuscate hospital pricing data is the only reason reference-based pricing (RBP) exists today. Hospital systems push back hard on these programs, often sending out memos across the hospital system and employer groups indicating they will not treat patients unless they have a traditional PPO plan or pay cash. This is illegal, but with endless financial resources (most are tax-payer-supported non-profits), they are comfortable doing what is most profitable.

The Brokers: Generally, insurance brokerages are paid by the large, fully insured carriers, with their compensation being "publicly" based on a percentage of premium. This means their compensation increases if the plan sponsor's insurance costs increase. No conflict of interest there. And how about those year-end bonuses for the largest broker-ages (not disclosed to employers) that make up a significant portion of their total revenue? Who is really the client?

The Large Fully Insured Carriers: Employers generally have a love-hate relationship with the big carriers. They love the simplicity of their offerings and appreciate the excellent customer service for their covered employees but hate the rate increases that erode their profit margins each year. So, to save money, a qualified employer will consider a self-funded plan option with the same carrier, referred to as an administrative services only (ASO) option. Their brokers will gener-ally support this to maintain their compensation structure with the carrier. The carrier will be pleased as well because they keep the busi-ness and still get to use the same vendor contracts and processes. It's the easy button, with employees none the wiser.

LOWERING TREND

With all the major fully insured carriers indicating trends in the 8-12 percent range, the opportunity cost of embracing transparent, value-based health plans becomes more appealing. Simply put, something must change because the current system has priced middle-class America out of coverage.

Change can be disruptive, but it is manageable, especially when members get better access to quality healthcare while lowering their out-of-pocket cost. A thoughtful plan design can do this, lowering a plan sponsors insurance cost and reducing their annual trend to 1-3 percent.

Recommendations:

- Don't ignore the numbers. If your insurance carrier is telling you the price of goods and services on your group health plan (trend) is going to increase by 8-12 percent over the next 12 months, believe them! Get mad, then channel that frustration into fuel for change.

- Seek to understand and resolve the conflicts of interest! Once you understand the challenges, this generally means changing vendors and working with a fee-based insurance producer willing to sign a conflict-of-interest statement. With vendors, there is a general rule of thumb: if you have never heard of them, they are probably doing something right.

You must:

- Have a clean pharmacy benefit manager (PBM) contract that eliminates all the "dumb" drugs (anything that may be considered a lifestyle drug, excessively priced and/or with questionable efficacy), clawbacks (when a plan's copay is set higher than the drug cost itself), and other conflicts of interest. This can be either a direct contract written by an independent consultant or for a smaller employer that lacks leverage. This allows the employer to "join" an existing contract being shared with other employers.
- Mandate the use of Centers of Excellence for many elective (non-emergency) procedures such as musculoskeletal (MSK), organ transplants, and other high-cost medical procedures. Ironically, the higher quality health providers generally cost less. Participating members will generally get their cost-sharing waived for participating, and many times, performance guarantees can be included for the procedure. If there is a problem with the procedure, the facility and the providers are held responsible.
- Lastly, support "independent" physician practices! Patients trust doctors, and Direct Primary Care (DPC) programs with self-employed primary care doctors are one of the best tools in the market for improving access to care, the patient experience, and clinical outcomes.

Unlike Wall Street, trend is not your friend, and a plan sponsor can no longer sit back waiting for the big, fully insured carriers, hospital systems, and politicians to solve the problem. As an entrepreneur and business owner, you must manage your healthcare plan the same way you do with the primary activities of your business. You must take control and manage your expenses! If you do not, the status quo will continue to do it for you until they price you out of any meaningful coverage.

---

1. Milliman. (2013).*Comparing Episode of Cancer Care Cost in Different Settings: An Actuarial Analysis of Patients Receiving Chemotherapy.* Milliman.
2. Peckham, Carol. (2018). *Medscape Oncologist Compensation Report 2018.* Medscape.
3. William, S., Rogstad, T., & Parekh, N. (2019). Waste in the US Health Care System. *JAMA Network.*

CHAPTER 6
HIGH SCHOOL CLIQUES & HEALTH INSURANCE

TRENT HARPER

This is your backstage pass to join those that do fully-insured to self-funding conversions every day.

———

DO you remember high school cliques? In all honesty, if you are reading this anthology, there are only so many of those groups that you probably fall into. Regardless, for this purpose, we will make believe that there were just two cliques—those who drove to school and those who walked. Then we will try and draw parallels between the world of providing healthcare benefits to your employees and the two paths before you: traditional first-dollar insurance or self-insurance.

If you had a choice to drive or walk to school, the in-crowd would undoubtedly be the drivers. Why would you walk? Is it a convincing enough argument that it is healthier? You certainly would have more flexibility in how you get to school, as far as which path you take. There is probably more variability in your surroundings along the way —trees, grass, and shrubbery, which is a positive. Indeed, it would be cheaper than gas and car payments, but it takes effort. Walking is certainly not easier than driving. It doesn't seem as efficient, and it takes time. Plus, who cares about being healthier because of those potential, long-term benefits when you can reap the short-term benefits in front of you now?

Though not a perfect analogy, self-insurance is like walking to school, while the easier, fully-insured route is like driving to school. For someone who has spent their whole career trying to sell the concept of self-insurance, this doesn't cast self-insurance in the best light. The process of adequately investigating and converting your health plan to a self-insured model is inefficient—it takes time and effort and requires an advisor who knows what they are doing (not just *saying* they know what to do). However, for most employers, given a five-year horizon, self-insurance will win out—plain and simple. If that is true, then why is it so inefficient? Why does it take so much more time and effort? Are there easier ways to get the same result?

I'm going to help you understand the barriers in the way of self-insurance and pick up on some interesting history and stats while giving you a little peek into why the healthcare industry (especially health insurance) is so messed up. I'm not trying to sell you what self-insurance is and why it might be the right fit for you here. You likely have some level of knowledge of the pros and cons of self-funding. This is your backstage pass to join those that do fully insured to self-funding conversions every day. So, put your keys down because it's time to walk.

Let's start with some history. Insurance had its beginnings in the coffee shops of seventeenth-century London. One was Edward Lloyd's little establishment by the River Thames. It became the center of marine intelligence and planted the seeds of modern insurance. Lloyd began renting boxes (tables) where ship owners could seek insurance in case they lost their cargo or their ship did not return. These ship owners would draft a document describing their ship, its contents, crew, and destination. Rate and terms were formulated and included in the document. Entrepreneurially minded businesspeople, who wished to assume some risk commitment, would sign their name at the bottom, specifying how much exposure they were willing to accept. This is where we get the word "underwriter"—those who wrote their name under the terms and rate. Through time, this association of ship owners and businessmen gained prominence. At one point in the late 1700s, Lloyd's organization knew of a British vessel captured by a French privateer (including lost cargo) before the British navy knew about it. As more insurance was written with more claims filed, the English law of maritime insurance was building a foundation for all types of insurance in the future. Today, Lloyds of London is the leading insurance and reinsurance marketplace worldwide.[1]

For those who aren't underwriters, basic insurance underwriting consists of two broad principles: selection of risk and spread of risk. Put on your seventeenth-century entrepreneur hat and think about these principles. Would you want to underwrite and insure a ship that was completely unknown to you, not knowing who built it, how long it's been around, how many voyages it's been on, what it was carrying, or where it was going? The selection of risk certainly matters. Assuming you have all your answers regarding risk selection, putting your money behind one ship will not bring much return in relation to the risk you are taking.

However, putting your name across multiple ships and cargo types brings reasonable predictability, thanks to the law of averages. Spread of risk matters as well. What is the balance between these two principles? Well, if you had some deep pockets and some very solid spread of risk (volume), you may be more inclined to skimp on your selection of risk principles. The vice versa is true as well. Without a strong spread of risk, you may find yourself much more selective in accepting your risk. In many ways, the more data you have about the risk you have underwritten, as well as the data about the potential new risk you may have yet to underwrite, the better. You can imagine that data can help you immensely in making these decisions. It's important to remember that Lloyd's was not just an insurance marketplace hub but a center of intelligence and information.

Let's contrast that against the current healthcare insurance environment in America. Most employers have no idea what risk they currently hold, especially if you are considered a small group employer. Why are your rates going up? Is it justified? How much did you spend on medical and prescription services recently? How much of that spend were large, high-dollar claims? What was the underlying diagnosis of those large claims? What is the prognosis? Will those continue to claim into your next benefit year? These are all great questions. Maybe, more importantly, is the question behind the question: why do health insurance carriers not share this data? If you are big enough, most states and carriers will have some level of data available (there are still some holdouts even if you are a large group employer). Data is cheap, right? If the carrier can put together dashboard summaries with high-level stats and benchmarks, it should have specific data to see if your company is a good selection of risk, correct? Of course, the answer is yes, but that doesn't mean these insurers share that with you or your advisor.

As an underwriter of employee benefit-risk, the biggest hurdle, hands down, is the lack of data supporting the selection of risk. Just like an unknown ship with unknown cargo and an unknown destination, if you, as the employer, are in the dark as to the utilization and specific high-cost diagnosis in your population, then that leaves me, as an underwriter, with nothing in that selection of risk column. The only principle underwriters have left is spread of risk. How does that work in this situation? We rely on an actuarial underwriting manual.

Think of it as a massive spreadsheet with millions of data points purchased from hospital systems, fully insured health insurers, networks, etc. The job of the actuary is then to take all those data points and essentially estimate the average cost of healthcare in a particular area for a given gender and age. The more lives I must underwrite or the more lives I have underwritten, the more likely I will hit those averages (law of averages). Hence, for me to leave behind the principle of selection of risk, I will need a lot more money to put at risk across a lot more people to hit my spread of risk. Who can you think of that has gobs of money and many benefit plan participants? That's right—the fully insured carriers. They hold back the data to create an environment where they are the only ones to achieve this risk spread. What can employers do?

Are you an excellent candidate for self-funding? Will you save money, or are you bleeding claims? The only way to know for sure is to be in the right state with the right carrier to get the experience reports needed or have your employees complete individual health questionnaires. Now you can start to see how this analogy of walking vs. riding in the car is beginning to take a little more shape. Walking takes more time and effort—but you will know once you go down that path, it won't be a question anymore. The data is yours, and the selection of risk principle finally comes back into play, not only for you but for the panoply of potential medical stop-loss options out there for you.

Now, let's assume you can get the data, whether from experience reports or medical questionnaires. Your part is now somewhat done, and you expect your broker/advisor to send that in so you can start to see some quotes. Analyses are coming your way; answers are finally at your fingertips. But there is a problem. Did you know there is absolutely no standardization on the employee benefits side of insurance? The various parties involved in sharing data to generate a proposal or analysis have no standard way of sharing that data in any form or fashion that is even remotely close to a uniform methodology. The easiest way to describe this is to compare and contrast.

I will simplify insurance into two broad categories: life/health and property/casualty. Life and health are where employee benefits fall. Property and casualty include your workers' compensation, general liability, commercial auto, property, crop insurance, etc. On the property and casualty side of insurance (P&C), there is an organization called ACORD, which stands for the Association for Cooperative Operations Research and Development. They are a non-profit global standard-setting body with a defined purpose of helping the industry acquire, synthesize, process and deliver data—to each other. They started in 1970, with the first paper forms available in 1972, enabling the flow of data across P&C insurance stakeholders. They currently have over twelve hundred standardized transaction types, from notices of loss, certificates of insurance, and applications for coverage, plus hundreds of state-specific forms (because the business of insurance is all at the state level, not federal). All of this across all major P&C lines of business. This means if you were looking to get a quote for workers' compensation insurance, your broker would use an

ACORD 130 form. It is already built into the computer system her insurance agency uses. She can send that out to her MGAs (managing general agents) and carriers, who all know what that form is. They all accept it. In fact, they could not get you a quote without that form. And to boot, all workers' compensation carriers produce loss runs—a history of all your workers' compensation claims. This happens no matter what size company you have. Not only are P&C carriers using the selection of risk principle, but they are also much faster, more accurate, and more efficient with this standardization of how data flows between all applicable groups and organizations.

There is no standard for formatting a census in the employee benefits space. A census is a document (usually a spreadsheet) that lists all eligible health plan members and their demographic information. Several times a week, my team works with an advisor or third-party administrator (TPA) to get just enough information on a census to start the analysis. Every census is different. How your plan design is laid out and described (what copays, coinsurances, etc.) is different from carrier to carrier. There is no standard application with basic information about your company, such as name, address, industry, etc. Essentially, there is no uniformity at all. However, the underwriting system we have indeed expects data in a particular way. That means almost everything we do must be manually typed in. The only exception is the census. What we do there is manipulate and copy and paste the submitted census into a format that can be uploaded into our underwriting platform. This process takes time, and it is not efficient. Compared to the fully insured carriers that have filed rates, built to essentially focus on that spread of risk vs. selection of risk concept, the self-funded employee benefits world looks slow and inefficient. Some platforms allow your broker to get a bindable, fully insured quote across dozens of plans and applicable carriers in your area within minutes. As a broker, it would be hard not to tilt towards the easy and recommend to you, as the client, to ride the car to school. Walking takes longer, with more effort, and the broker compensation is pretty much the same, if not less, when you choose to take that stroll (self-fund).

We may need to stop here and investigate why it is this way. Many anthologies could probably be written about that question. But right off the bat, we can say that the P&C insurance industry has more carriers (over 2,500 to 900 health insurance carriers). So, wouldn't it be harder to wrangle all those P&C carriers together to cooperate and set standards? It is hard to pinpoint any reason or cause why health insurance is seemingly so much more inefficient. And that is certainly not to say that P&C insurance is the bee's knees. There are plenty of areas for improvement, and they are nowhere near a perfect model.

But in comparison, these two sides of insurance have quite the divide. Available data vs. no data, standards vs. no standards, and probably most interesting, options vs. consolidation. The health insurance world has seen a significant move towards consolidation. Just five carriers account for 169 million covered Americans. In the industry, we have an acronym for that – BUCAH (*boo-ka*). It represents the major fully insured carriers, Blue Cross/Blue Shield (Anthem), United, Cigna, Aetna, and Humana.

Consolidation is when two or more companies join forces or combine. Generally, they used to be competitors, but now through mergers or acquisitions, they are one larger company. In insurance, it is interesting because it often looks like different names and policies, but it's the same parent conglomerate. Insurance carriers will have writing companies and segments based on geography, past mergers, and acquisitions, where a particular name or carrier stays put while still falling under the larger parent company (like when CVS acquired Aetna). This consolidation can be vertical – such as a health plan merging with a hospital system, or horizontal – two hospitals or two insurers merging. There is a commonly accepted measure of market concentration called the Herfindahl-Hirschman Index (HHI). The federal government will use the HHI score in a particular market as part of its evaluation for approving potential mergers. If a score is less than 1,500, that market is considered competitive and not concentrated. A score between 1,500 and 2,500 would be considered moderately concentrated. A score above 2,500 is considered highly concentrated and not competitive. Using this rubric, 70 percent of metropolitan statistical areas have health plans that are rated as highly concentrated, as reported by the American Medical Association. Even in hospitals, 80 percent of metro statistical areas are rated highly concentrated. The concern is that when there is too much concentration and not enough competition among healthcare facilities or benefit plans, one side has too much leverage, resulting in rising prices and potentially reduced quality in healthcare. Further, I would posit that consolidation does not lead to innovation or cooperation in the overall industry. It means that anyone trying to break the traditional mold and offer employers something different must contend with the natural protectionism symptoms that can come with such consolidation.

Though it's not *the* smoking gun or *the* only factor, consolidation certainly seems like at least a reasonable explanation and starting point for the lack of improvement, standardization, and data in the employer benefit space. Consolidation contributes to why self-insurance continues to take longer and looks so inefficient. I can't help to feel marginalized against the "cool crowd," the clique that has it all—the cool cars, the air conditioning, and all the free time before school. Like a high school clique, it's hard to leave. It is hard to abandon the "in group." The BUCAHs have a pretty good stranglehold on the market. Why would you want to be in the walking clique? It is time, effort, and a struggle to decide if it is even worth the hassle of going down that road. Honestly, it is unclear whether brokers or advisors understand all this. The incentives are to follow the path of least resistance.

There are many alternatives to our selection of risk conundrum that service providers and brokers want to employ because it is so difficult to get good data out of fully insured carriers. But nothing beats actual data. And how wonderful would it be if that data was standardized to flow freely in the open marketplace amongst all applicable stakeholders? The long-term benefits of walking outweigh driving, even though it is more painful. And there are times and situations when driving is the only option. If you have a broken foot, get in the car!

As a whole, the industry is antiquated and lacks innovation, competition, and options. At the very least, as the employer, you should be allowed to be empowered to go in with eyes wide open and understand your most expensive financial expenditures—employee benefits. Until that moment comes, the next time you have the choice between your fully insured option and looking at a self-funded alternative, you at least know a little bit more about what is happening behind the curtain. Give yourself some time and be patient but know at the very least that it will be a learning experience. Oh, and ask your broker how they are getting to school.

---

1. Lloyd's Coffee and commerce: Travels through our history

CHAPTER 7
SELF-FUND OR DIE

SPENCER SMITH

Once you open yourself up to the world of self-funding, the opportunities become limitless to tinker with and solve problems.

───────

IF YOU ARE READING this book, you probably play some role in helping run an organization. Whether you are in the C-Suite, adjacent, or have 50 or 500 employees on staff, you are likely aware that your health plan is one of the most significant line items on your profit and loss report. I will also take a wild guess and assume you are fully insured. Fully insured means you buy insurance from a carrier, typically Blue Cross, United, Cigna, Aetna, or Humana (BUCAH), and transfer all your health claim risk to them in exchange for a premium. Simplifying it even more, you pay the carrier premium, and regardless of what healthcare your employees consume throughout the plan year, that carrier pays for it if the person and the claim are eligible. You don't have to think about it. It's the easy button.

You're running a business; you don't have time for this health insurance crap, right? Wrong. The problem with being fully insured is that you are typically in the dark about what is driving your health insurance costs. Is it the over-utilization of emergency room care? Is it the high cost of prescription drugs? Do you have an imaging center in your small town raking your employees over the coals? When you are fully insured, answering these questions is difficult, if not impossible.

You have no insight, no control, and you get stuck on a merry-go-round of ever-increasing costs with very little ability to counteract that trend. In short, if you don't come up with a better solution, you're screwed. You won't retain your best employees, you won't attract the most talented employees to join your company, and ultimately, you will still pay out the nose for healthcare.

By staying fully insured year after year, you only have a few levers to pull to try and offset the cost increases over time. You can change carriers, chase lower rates, and/or reduce the quality of your health plan, but all of those choices ultimately punish your employees with higher costs and worse benefits.

All right. Sweet. Thank you, Spencer, for hammering home my problem, but what the hell do I do? The answer is self-funding your health plan. To self-fund, your health plan (*partially* self-fund, but I won't bore you with semantics) means that instead of paying a carrier premium in exchange for *all* the claim risk, you as an employer decide to self-fund your claims risk up to specified levels. You pick a medical third-party administrator (TPA) or a Pharmacy Benefit Manager (PBM), and you buy something called stop-loss insurance from a carrier. Now, the stop-loss carrier sets a limit (like a deductible). As the employer, all claim expenses under that stop-loss limit are your responsibility to pay. The carrier pays any claims that exceed that limit. This differs from a fully-insured model, where the carrier pays all claims in exchange for your premium.

Rather than prepaying, you get the opportunity to pay claims as they come in. When you prepay claims, if the cost of your premiums is $1 million a year, but your company only incurs $500,000 of claims, then you just overpaid by $500,000 for your risk because the insurer keeps the difference. I promise that at renewal, that carrier will not give you 50 percent off the previous year's rates! No, they're going to talk about how their overall risk pool is performing poorly and how they need a 9 percent increase for your insurance to cover their increasing costs. They don't tell you they are fine with increasing costs because they know they can increase their rates yearly. With fixed medical loss ratio requirements, the only way they can make more money is for the absolute costs of claims to go up, but that is a different story for another book!

However, let's consider the example above if you, as an employer, are self-funded. In that same year, since you only had $500,000 in claims, but had set a budget of $1 million for your healthcare based on your projected spend, the remaining $500,000 in funds are yours to keep. Any surplus in funding that wasn't spent on claims belongs to you. You now have an opportunity to win that you didn't have before, even if it's not guaranteed. And who doesn't at least want the *opportunity* to win? Being self-funded gives you the *opportunity*!

Saving money is often the most significant factor in why an employer decides to self-fund, but multiple factors influence this decision. Here are a few of the primary ones:

They reach a specific size: With around 100-200 enrolled employees, most employers traditionally start exploring becoming self-funded, or their benefits consultant suggests it to them. There are plenty of smaller employers who decide to self-fund. Still, when employers reach this size threshold (100-200 employees), their risk becomes more predictable, making their businesses more stable. They also have dedicated employees who evaluate their benefits throughout the year.

Stable cash flow: This is something my friend Dennis Fowler calls the "EKG effect." An employer needs to have predictable and adequate cash flow. The EKG effect is due to the fluctuations in claims costs that employers pay when they self-fund. The rise and fall of claims month to month mimics the peaks and valleys of an EKG monitoring a patient's heart rate. Having stable cash flow means you are prepared for the larger-than-average claim that will invariably arise once you are self-funding. You can use mechanisms to mitigate your worst-case scenario risk through stop-loss. Still, regardless of the cap, you must be prepared for unpredictability in your monthly claims spend and have adequate funds allocated.

They want control: Employers seeking more choices and autonomy pursue self-funding. When fully insured, you must choose between a few carriers in your market and only from plan designs filed by carriers in your state. When you self-fund, you get a broader array of vendors allowing you to mix and match components of a plan at each renewal rather than making wholesale changes from carrier to carrier. You also get more flexibility in your plan design and what networks you can access, even having the ability to use something called "reference-based pricing" (Medicare as the benchmark to pay claims) or direct contracts with providers.

They want data: The adage says that "you cannot manage what you cannot measure," and being fully insured means you have little or no claims data to measure. How can you lower the cost of your health plan if you have no idea where your money goes? Fully insured carriers limit claims data for small, fully insured groups, which leaves these groups in the dark as to why renewal increases keep coming. This creates a competitive moat, making it harder for you to leave them. When you are self-funded, you get significantly more data, mainly if you use an independent third-party administrator (TPA). Monthly aggregate reports, extensive claims reports, pending/denied claims, pre-certification reports, and case management notes are all part of the common claims package when self-funded. Once you have this data, you have the power to alter the outcomes of your future plan-spend!

Lower administrative costs: Finally, employers want to reduce their fixed costs. When you self-fund, you separate the fixed costs from the variable costs of claims. This means that the portion that is genuinely fixed each month for premium administration costs, taxes, etc., is a fraction of what it is when fully insured because the variable costs of claims become its bucket of funds. Then you can focus on controlling your destiny by uncovering what drives the variable portion and set out to correct it. For this reason alone, it is enough motivation for many employers to self-fund.

The reasons to self-fund listed above are not exhaustive but speak to the most common motivations. Once you open yourself up to the world of self-funding, the opportunities become limitless to tinker with and solve problems. You can explore adding direct primary care for your employees, which offers a fixed-cost model for primary care delivery that simultaneously provides members higher quality care with more physician accessibility. You can carve out certain conditions, like transplants or dialysis, or find a PBM that helps you source the more costly specialty medications overseas or through dedicated government programs. If you are self-funded and get a bad stop-loss insurance renewal, you can change just your stop-loss carrier rather than make wholesale changes to the entire plan. The possibilities are endless, but very few of the abovementioned solutions are available without being self-funded.

Now, as a business owner, maybe you have been told by your consultant that you are not suitable for self-funding. Perhaps you have been told you are too small, your risk profile is too bad, or it will create a more administrative burden on your staff. While some of these things may be partially true, chances are that these objections offered by your broker/adviser/consultant might be biased.

Often, insurance brokers lack the necessary education to help you plan and manage a self-funded plan. It also creates more work for them. And lastly, perhaps they might deter you from exploring this funding mechanism because it often leads to less revenue for your broker. If your agent is being paid commissions to manage your health plan, the agent will potentially experience a dramatic drop in their income when you reduce your premium by self-funding. Commissions are a function of premium, so if premiums go down (unless they precipitously raise their commission percentage to offset this drop), they will probably make less money on the same account.

Therefore, many of the most innovative brokers will either charge a flat fee to manage your plan or tie their revenue to a successful outcome of your health plan. Either way, I strongly recommend working with a consultant to manage your health plan on a net-of-commission arrangement, to ensure proper alignment of incentives for both parties.

CHAPTER 8
LIABILITY BY ASSOCIATION

AMY HOWARD

Most employers do not always understand that they hold a lot of liability, even when they have stop-loss coverage.

———

STOP-LOSS and self-funding benefit plans have been marketed as the next great thing for controlling costs. Having more control of your health plan and rate stabilization are just a few benefits of self-funding. These benefits are all true, to a point. When changing from a fully insured program to a self-funded one, there are many things to consider. For an insurance model that touts the transparency of the product, it is a wonder how employers have not yet discovered the dark underbelly of stop-loss policies. There is a lot of liability and risk in making that move, and you must do a lot of self-reflection, face some hard truths about your risk tolerance, and seriously look at the people and companies helping you make decisions.

The pitfalls of self-insurance and stop-loss are rarely explained to employers. Those pitfalls and the possibility of additional liability have significant consequences. You must trust your employees, a high-quality administrator, and have confidence in your advisors. Following the wrong lead can cost you money, employees, and your business.

Employers must educate themselves, knowing enough to be dangerous, not necessarily subject matter experts, regarding basic benefit plans and stop-loss insurance. Know the difference between the funding mechanisms of fully insured, traditional self-funding, and level funding and the difference between working with a large carrier and a smaller one. Most importantly, know the math! It may sound basic, but once you understand the concepts of stop-loss and self-funding, it is all a math game. These little bits of knowledge could save you thousands of dollars.

I work primarily with small employers, with groups under 100 lives. Most are first-time self-funders, lured by the promise of transparency, cost containment, control, and ultimately money back in their pockets. I have seen small-group employers thrive with this model, saving money, giving employees better benefits at a lesser cost, and watching their businesses grow. I have also seen employers who lost using this model, even shutting their doors or being purchased by bigger companies.

It can be quite overwhelming for a first-timer to dive into this world. It will sometimes feel like the wild west as self-funding opens many opportunities to change benefits, funding mechanisms, and overall communication with employees. Getting lost in a maze of regulations (or lack thereof), decisions, and data is easy. Most employers do not always understand that they hold a lot of liability, even with stop-loss coverage. Large holes in coverage may go unnoticed—for example, contract types, plan and policy exclusions, and underwriting assumptions. I have been a first-hand witness to all these things, and when things go badly, the employer suffers. The best way to protect yourself would be to understand different kinds of contracts, what they cover, and where the gaps could be. Plan and policy exclusions are typically standard within the self-funded world, but if the policy you are purchasing is stricter than your plan, you could have gaps. We underwrite our groups using individual health questionnaires (IHQs). IHQs are necessary when there isn't enough historical claims data available to examine and underwrite a group. These are great underwriting tools as you get more up-to-date information from those receiving the treatment. That is, until something is missed.

This is where the trust in employees comes into play. Communication is key. When asking employees to complete these forms, I have always been baffled that the reasons there needs to be full disclosure are not relayed to those completing the forms. I repeatedly hear that the employee was worried they would be charged more premium or just denied coverage. This thinking is something that needs to be addressed and changed. If employees knew and understood that completing these forms in their entirety, truthfully and timely, could save their employer and themselves thousands of dollars, they would be motivated to be thorough and honest. Individual health questionnaires that contain some higher-risk individuals may cause an underwriter to pause and increase a rate by a few points. Still, those dollars are small compared to that one employee who was not honest, causing the carrier to deny their large claims. The employer is left with a hard decision to make.

As an employer, it is always wise to be familiar with the fine print on IHQs. Those forms may allow the plan to deny claims for dishonesty, but not all of them do. Even with this right, employers are left with a very difficult choice of enforcement. If it is decided to deny all the claims, it could cause employees to leave and find other employment. If it is decided to pay these claims, it could seriously cost or even bankrupt the group depending on how expensive the claims are, because they would not be covered under the stop-loss policy. Also, when making such a decision, it isn't just for that one employee who has been with the company for twenty-plus years; it is for *all* employees because you are setting a precedent. These precedents must. be offered to all employees, regardless of tenure or status within the company, or the employer could face discrimination lawsuits.

Having trust in your administrator is imperative. It is essential to conduct an exhaustive search for an administrator that is not just licensed but also has the same philosophies in health insurance. Your administrator has the power to cause chaos within your employee base, cause employees to leave your company, or make the administration of your benefit plan run smoothly. They influence your employees' decisions to stay with your company over competitive offers from others because they love the benefits package and experience.

How does one pick an administrator? That is a complex process, and you need to be ready to ask some tough questions to understand what it takes to service a health plan fully. The biggest issue that employers have with administrators is financial. An administrator who does not understand financial systems, requirements, and consequences could result in additional charges for taxes, fees, and penalties. Also, you could end up paying other compensation (commissions, kickbacks, overrides) to your administrator and your advisor. Take a long look at what services your administrator offers, get examples of reporting, and find out what is included in their fees. Sometimes the most expensive administrators are not the best. Bigger is not always better, either!

Your administrator is usually your first and sometimes only line of defense against fraud, malpractice, and other negligent claims against your health plan. Administrators typically become fiduciary of the program—in the simplest terms, they have the right to direct plan assets (your money). Accurate claim payments and a solid auditing process of those payments are paramount to your success as a self-funded health plan. Claims not paid in accordance with the plan document are one of the biggest reasons for a stop-loss carrier to deny claims.

Your administrator should treat your plan assets as though they were paying for those claims out of their account. You want to look for an administrator with a good track record of keeping year-over-year costs (or what we call trend) low, and you also want to examine how that is done. Do they look at all claims for possible subrogation? Do they look at claims of dependents for the possibility of other insurance? Do they look at their vendors regularly to ensure they are paying (and passing the cost along to you) the best price for those services?

Administrators should also have a good record of customer service. Your employees and their providers will interact with your administrator almost daily. Having a well-educated and experienced customer service team and administrator will make your employees feel taken care of by their insurance plan and employer. Poor customer service is a killer, any way you cut it. When an administrator does not have good customer service, it is very easy for your employees to see you, the employer, coming between the care they need and the doctor providing it.

Most newcomers to the self-funded arena hire an advisor of some kind. They can be consultants or brokers, but you need to know the difference and what is right for you. The right advisor is a game changer in the world of self-funded health plans. You should rely on this person to be the expert and assist you in navigating the complex world of self-funding. All of them promise to save you money, but a good advisor will, while the wrong one will cost you. For things to run smoothly, working with the right advisor should be a team effort. You will see month-over-month savings, which rapidly add up. Advisors are *not* cheap, and the cost doesn't always correlate with quality—just like everything else these days. To pick a good advisor, research, ask questions, and ask for references (both current and past clients). Do not be afraid to be forceful by demanding and expecting answers that prove their worth. Many advisors are out there, and they all want business. You must recognize that you are the one holding power. Use it wisely.

CHAPTER 9
THE COMPANY YOU KEEP

DR. MADELINE SMITH

*The cost of your insurance and your members' satisfaction directly correspond
to the broker you have.*

————

IN MY EXPERIENCE, there are three types of brokers: the Greedy
Bastards, the Clueless, and the Good Samaritans.

THE GREEDY BASTARDS

The Greedy Bastards dominate the industry. Some have been around
since the true beginning of group health insurance (or modern medicine) it feels like. They are accustomed to making six or seven figures a
year in exchange for a few hours of "work" a week, but mostly in
exchange for lifelong social relationships that guarantee them Broker
of Record on large accounts. There is no pressure to save their clients'
money, no pressure to provide creative solutions, just an annual exercise in "marketing" the group to carriers while trying to find the best
deal. Finding the best deal involves pitting carriers against each other,
trying to see who's willing to lowball the rates enough to win the business, only to increase them the following year.

No love loss from me here; it's not like the carriers are hurting for cash or are sponsoring a charitable fund. But it's not work. It's manipulating the players so you can show the client what great, exhaustive work you did for them and how it dramatically reduced their costs. It's a regular practice now, particularly in the fully insured world. Let's say the carrier releases a 28% increase, intending to come down to 2% when they enter the negotiation phase with the broker. This process isn't unique to Greedy Bastards. It's the way they respond that entitles them to the title. Their fees are usually baked into the cost of insurance. It's a commission that increases when the client's cost increases. Commission-based income isn't specific to health insurance. It's common in the sales world. But think about the difference in dynamics.

When we walk into a car dealership, we know we are being sold something. We know we aren't paying the salesman/woman directly. We know the dealership is paying them when we buy something. Health insurance is different, though. The broker is said to work for the client—the employer. But they are paid by the carrier. When the carrier increases the premium, and the employer's costs go up, the broker gets a raise. How does that make sense? New disclosure laws mandate (somewhat vaguely) that they must disclose what funds and from whom they receive them, but even that has some loopholes. Up to this point, much of the commission isn't disclosed, is done on regulatory filings, or in size four font footnoted at the bottom of paperwork. CEOs and CFOs typically wouldn't fall for this in any other area of their lives. Most don't realize this is the game. Or… they have golfed with their broker for twenty years and couldn't imagine the personal conflict if they demanded something else. Most employers aren't equipped with enough facts or insights about their group, risk profile, performance, and cost to fight back. Buying from this type of broker and complaining about healthcare being too expensive doesn't make sense. No one from this category will catch slack from me. Greedy. Fucking. Bastards.

THE CLUELESS

While the industry is complex, being an agent or broker doesn't require that you become an expert. There are many with impressive careers based on having sufficient knowledge to service their clients. Sufficient knowledge can mean familiarity with a few products and carriers and good working relationships with a handful of carrier reps. A top-notch customer service or account management team makes up for any lack of insight or expertise. Because all too often, the buyer (the employer) isn't sure what they need, their options, or what to ask. It's possible to skate through with basic awareness of the industry. These broker relationships can be classified as "sell it and forget it." I'm not suggesting that The Clueless can't do good work or that what they provide isn't in the client's best interest, but it's just sufficient. Many are paid under the same flawed percentage of the premium model only because they've never considered another way. If clients asked to be paid as a fixed fee, they would be open to it. When told about a new product or solution, they look into it but aren't seeking it out. When asked a question they can't answer, they research it, but they aren't proactively learning or expanding their knowledge base.

THE GOOD SAMARITANS

These guys/gals are one of the only reasons I have stayed in the business and have broker clients. They are dramatically the minority. Many never intended to be in this business. The ones I've met have come from other areas. Some wanted to go to medical school but didn't. Some started in another area of insurance, risk, or service and accidentally ended up in sales/consulting. Others inherited their parents' businesses and wanted to change the agency's trajectory. Some Good Samaritans are disruptive as hell, challenging the norms and publicly calling out the inequities they see in the industry. They are loud and unafraid of the fallout that will come from their messages. Many Good Samaritans are represented on these pages.

Others are less aggressive and silently do the good work. They are putting together real solutions for clients, constantly educating themselves, and trying to serve their employer clients and members the best way they know how. What is frustrating is how hard this industry is for the good guys. Everything is working against them. If they charge a reasonable (disclosed) fee for the work they know they are doing, it's only a matter of time before a large Greedy Bastards firm comes in with shiny reports and the promise of the "big firm" expertise to steal their client. If they put creative plans together that save the members and employer money, those plans are often more work for them while paying the same. If they try to grow their agencies, expand their footprint, or partner with new vendors or carriers, they are met with questions about how much volume they can bring. The *how* of what they do is overlooked. And yet, they persevere. They are the last good thing about this industry, and I pray they don't give up and continue to find partners and clients who recognize them for their work and philosophy.

SO WHAT?

You probably already know which category your advisor falls in. I'm not here to preach about what you should expect or put up with. But we can't ignore that the cost of your insurance and your members' satisfaction directly correspond to the broker you have. The cost is affected because your broker impacts what they do with your group plans. What you hear about, what vendors and products you learn about, and what carriers or reinsurance you work with are all controlled by your broker.

Are they showing you the products that make the most sense for your specific group, or are they offering you the solutions that pay them the most? Are they getting a volume bonus by putting multiple clients on the same products? Is it easier for their staff to support one or two products or vendors/carriers, so that's all you see? Is their work ultimately client-centric, or is everything broker-centric? These questions and considerations can directly affect your bottom line. You must be able to see the most cost-effective solutions for your group.

There are other nuanced impacts as well: what are they missing? What is getting missed if they are not in the weeds with you, looking out for things? You probably are not looking at every report (although some of you do). What plan provisions do you have that are costing you more than they should? What coverages are you missing that might eventually cost you less (i.e., telemedicine), or what are you covering that you shouldn't? This comes down to the broker you have. How did you select them? How often do you evaluate them? Did you determine they were the right fit because of their philosophy and service or the products they put in front of you?

Remember that most brokers and agencies can get you access to the same products. The real question is how they support those products. Picking a broker or agency should be more of a philosophical question than a product or rates question. The most successful client/broker relationships are founded on a philosophical alignment, not a sale of a product or a presentation of rates. Many clients don't like to switch brokers midyear and instead take their plans to request for proposal (RFP) alongside their renewal. I have found this a flawed approach.

First, it's too much chaos. You're changing a lot: your broker, your support team, and potentially your benefits (network, carrier, pharmacy program, etc.). You are also not getting the most truthful, authentic version of the new brokers who pitch themselves to you. They are negotiating *hard*. They are calling in favors with their carriers, doing everything they can to show you the lowest rates and richest benefits they can muster. Notice there's never a multiyear rate lock (unless you're talking about non-health benefits). They can't lock it in. They are giving you the best they've got to win the business.

I would recommend something else. Take your broker/agency to RFP midyear when you have no plans to change anything. This accomplishes a few things. First, you are giving them no ability to sell products or solutions—they must win your business strictly based on merit. They must wow you with their knowledge, philosophy, customer support, and operating modes. Tell them you are looking for them to come in and support your existing products. You can determine quickly who comes in and tries to pitch you alternative strategies. There's nothing wrong with this because perhaps you need a change or improvement. It can give you a window into who and what they are promoting and if it's genuinely to fill a need of yours or if they are trying to grow their volume with a particular product or carrier. This strategy gives you, your team, your employees, and their families time to get to know the agency and their team. There's a low-stress time for everyone to work together and hopefully build rapport and trust. Finally, it gives a good broker a genuine opportunity to determine what is working and what isn't based on your current offerings. An RFP is helpful and necessary, but I would compare it to a scenario where you buy a used car and go for a test drive. If you jump behind the wheel, turn a few corners, and come back to the dealer, you know a few things. The car starts, drives, turns, and the lights work. But if it's summer, you probably didn't try the heat (or if winter, you probably didn't try the air). You do not know how it drives on the highway. Allowing your new broker to get to know your members and see what's working and what isn't is giving them a week with your new, used car. Let them see it all so they are more equipped to make genuine recommendations. It also allows them to evaluate your appetite for risk or disruption.

Everything I've outlined here is an obvious overgeneralization of the people in the broker/agency world. There are great people within all firms; on some level, it's unfair of me to paint them all with the same brush. But… the dynamics I've outlined here are real, and you can bet they have a dramatic and tangible impact on your bottom line. You must decide if you'll keep complaining about how expensive healthcare is or will you take a good, hard look at whom you've selected to help you purchase it. It's not always pleasant and may feel like something you don't have time for. Trust me; you can no longer afford not to.

CHAPTER 10
NOTHING IN LIFE IS FREE

PAUL CARTER

The only thing we, as consumers, purchase in our lives that we don't know the actual cost of is medical and pharmacy services.

———

I HAD an epiphany as I read the title of this anthology. Although a small army of people throughout the country fully realize how the financing of America's healthcare system is tremendously flawed, many others like to complain about it and never actually do anything to address the problem. Here's what I mean.

Employers are often quick to admit they don't like how the current system works. They constantly complain about the lack of control, transparency, and out-of-control, spiraling costs. Many business owners realize the healthcare financing business model operates differently from other models and consumes a tremendous amount of corporate resources. They are left apprehensive about making meaningful changes within their program for fear of an employee revolt.

Conversely, many employers admit they don't like the current system and will do something about it. These employers have finally remembered a simple fact—they are the customer/consumer; their goals and needs should count! Wow, that's a liberating statement! It all seems so simple for those who have spent the better part of their careers addressing the pitfalls of healthcare financing.

A few realities must be acknowledged to truly address the unsustainable high cost of healthcare in the United States. First, the services that matter most from a cost perspective are facility-based services, high-cost diagnostics testing, dialysis services, medically inappropriate services, and provider billing errors. These are driving costs higher and must be addressed. Pharmacy costs, especially specialty pharmacy costs, require the same attention. We also must come together and insist that price transparency becomes the norm (i.e., knowing the costs of service before it's provided).

Amazing things can happen to healthcare costs by simply having the nerve (some feel audacity) to ask about the cost/price of the services. Let this statement sink in. The only thing we, as consumers, purchase *in our lives* that we don't know the actual cost of is medical and pharmacy services. To say this is flawed and leads directly to abusive behaviors is an understatement of epic proportions. Yet we have been "trained" to believe this is the norm and *must* be accepted.

Too many employers have been conditioned to believe these flaws cannot be addressed or corrected. Employees might revolt if faced with change. However, I firmly believe that if a company's current or future benefits program fails to address these issues, you're wasting your resources. I also think that the changes we make today will 100 percent be the norm ten to twenty years from now. Why? Because the way it's done, in a widespread manner today, doesn't make any sense.

So how do some organizations get to a place where they don't just complain but address the problems in meaningful ways? I believe these organizations share similar traits:

- Leadership leads the organization. Leaders don't delegate the essential functions of their businesses without providing their companies' overall direction and goals. Based on this leadership, they expect their senior staff to embrace the direction as their own and share or communicate it throughout the organization.

- They have accepted a simple notion of "I [business owner] can't do business that way; what makes them [carrier/provider] think they can?"
- They work with advisors/consultants who acknowledge and understand the organization's goals and work to provide solid options for those in leadership positions.

However, it should also be noted that just because organizations possess the characteristics listed above and implement innovative programs and services, there is no guarantee that the changes will be successful. In fact, many are not. Why? Once again, I feel the following specific traits are present:

- Leadership is bought into *what* the changes achieve, not *how* the changes are achieved.
- Leadership instructs Human Resources (HR) to implement the program yet fails to provide strong direction to ensure that HR fully understands the benefits associated with the program for both the company and its members. It is certainly not uncommon for the HR department's function to be a significant liability in how they "adopt" the program and how it's communicated to the employee membership.
- Leadership fails to ensure that their advisor and vendors take a hands-on, active role in the implementation process. The completely ridiculous passive enrollment process is a particular nail in the coffin of these types of programs. If the plan is passive, it's best to stick with your carrier-based program and live with the results.

Hopefully, an overarching theme is evident here. Organizational leadership plays a critical part in the success of these programs. It is startling how often addressing such a significant part of a company is given such limited attention. I feel this is directly related to how we've all been "taught" to purchase healthcare services. Examples of this old-school mentality include:

- As consumers, we cannot ask what the total costs of services are before they are provided.
- As consumers, we have been conditioned to believe that the only part of the costs that matter is the member's out-of-pocket expenses. This ignores the actual total cost of the services. Does this make sense?
- As consumers, we have been taught to trust that the treating provider always has the member's best interest in mind. Anyone that's been placed in financial harm's way by their provider, who doesn't consider a member's health plan benefits, would undoubtedly disagree with this notion. Everyone must remember that the treating physician *is not* the person *paying* the bill. It may sound crass, but the financial part of healthcare needs to be included in these discussions.
- As consumers, we have been taught that the national carriers have a "difficult" relationship with the provider community. This story is regularly presented in the media. The fact is that both organizations want the same thing – the status quo. Now they may differ on how they want to achieve this lofty goal, but make no mistake, they both want it. They do not want members to feel empowered to discuss the financial aspect of healthcare. National carriers' and providers' authority is weakened when members do this. This central component must and *will* change over the next few years.

The bottom line is that medical providers want you to make a purchase—for many people, the second or third largest purchase they will make in their lifetime—and do so without having any idea of the cost. Imagine buying a car like this. Imagine going to a dealership to get the vehicle you need, then signing a large amount of paperwork without reading and understanding the documents. After, the dealer gives you the keys, and you leave with your new vehicle. Forty-five days later, you get a bill that says you owe $100,000 for a car that you know you bought for $25,000. Who, as a consumer, would ever do such a thing? The answer is anyone of us when we need medical services. This is the absurdity of the current healthcare system from a financial perspective.

Another question I am frequently asked is, "If there are so many terrific cost-saving programs available, why doesn't my insurance company use them?" I have two theories about this question. First, change causes discomfort, so it becomes too difficult. Why make changes or do anything substantive when they do not fear losing customers? Second, any program that claims to save money on healthcare yet fails to address the actual cost of it (what the providers get paid) isn't worth much. Non-carrier-based companies exist because they *do* save money. If they don't save money, they no longer exist. This is a business reality. However, when non-carrier-based organizations must control costs, the carriers must *calculate* the costs accurately. In other words, does it really matter to the carrier if they are overpaying for services when their clients are the ones paying? The reality is that the employer group and members pay for the higher costs. Ask yourself this question: "Is there a difference between doing the work to *control* the costs or simply doing the *math* correctly and passing on to the customer the results of the math?" I've spent the better part of my career believing there is.

There are truly remarkable, innovative options available today that address current industry deficiencies. Make no mistake; these options *will* save a significant amount of money for the plan and members. Frankly, anyone who tells you otherwise is not being truthful. Remember, the savings are the *what*. It is vital for all those involved to understand the *how*. The thought of doing things exactly like they are done today while still achieving substantial savings is a fallacy. I call it "magic." Unfortunately, in this line of work, we are forced to deal in math, not magic.

Employers must understand *how* the results are achieved. Embrace the *how* from the top down and ensure everyone receives the benefits the *how* produced. If you do these things, you are well on your way to a better health plan solution for your employees and their families.

CHAPTER 11
GETTING WHAT YOU DESERVE FROM YOUR BROKER AND THIRD PARTY ADMINISTRATOR (TPA)

DOUG SHERMAN

It is time to expect more from your broker.

———

THINK about how it feels when it is time for the health insurance annual renewal. It is not something you look forward to with eager expectations. You may have already given up on your employees' excitement about the new health benefit plans you were paying for long ago. You hope that they won't complain too much.

You are stuck with three seemingly immovable premises. First, health insurance typically goes up 8-20 percent a year. Second, you must offer good benefits to attract and retain employees. Third, health insurance is a line item in your operating expenses that you have no control over. Finally, when premiums go up each year, you either swallow hard and pay more or face the ugly and potentially dangerous strategy of employees paying increased out-of-pocket costs.

It is not uncommon for either the carrier or the third-party administrator (TPA) to create noise among your employees when medical bills are wrongly denied or delayed in payment, or the member has poor customer service and complains about it. You are left feeling stuck with what you have, not knowing another option. Undoubtedly, you have noticed that health insurance is one industry that has rising costs and declining value—a negative scissors effect.

Every company has an ethos on the spectrum of being *self-centric* or *customer-centric*, or somewhere in the middle. I call the poles of this spectrum the "S" or the "C" factor. High C-factor companies can articulate your needs better than you can. They innovate more than their peers in meeting your needs. They don't just sell good value propositions. They deliver on them with a superior customer experience. Here, they provide an intersection of a superior value proposition with excellence in delivery.

As an owner of a health insurance agency and a TPA, I believe the health insurance industry generally has high "S" and low "C" factors. Worse, many employers are convinced there are no other options than the status quo. Let's start by considering the broker for a moment.

ABOUT THE BROKER

You want your broker to work hard to shop benefits for you and find excellent health plan options with innovative cost-containment strategies for stable pricing. You want them to conduct enrollment education and to ensure the carrier or the TPA provides the member with the best customer experience possible.

If the broker is average, they believe in the adage, "if it ain't broke, don't fix it." Their goal is to get the renewal, not to offer anything that might risk your disapproval. Further, they have other clients and are convinced they have little time to go shopping for you to find better plans with genuinely innovative cost-containment strategies. The sad truth is that, like electricity, you must have health plans for your business, but brokers do not make more or less money if your needs are met or not. There is a rough similarity between many health insurance brokers and government employees (but there are outstanding exceptions!).

Many brokers are too afraid to suggest migrating from a fully funded plan to a level or self-funded plan. Many don't take the time to learn about self-funded plans and new cost-containment strategies. Second, brokers don't want to risk that you will not like the new plans and will fire them next year. They are banking that you, as the employer or HR professional, believe there is nothing better out there. The typical broker exemplifies the high "S" factor ethos. It is all about them and little about meeting your business or personal objectives.

ABOUT THE TPA OR CARRIER ADMINISTRATOR

But let's say you find the right broker with a high C-factor. Let's say they have recommended an excellent self-funded plan, found a good underwriter, lined up the best stop-loss carrier, and created a rich assortment of cost-containment strategies. Let's give them the highest C-factor score possible. They still have no control over the execution of this plan. That falls in the lap of a TPA or carrier. Go to a benefits convention and listen to their conversations. Soon, you will hear them outdo each other with terrible TPA or carrier operation stories that make them look bad and jeopardize their incomes.

So, let's consider some of your needs from the TPA or carrier operations. Here are some basics of what you want from the TPA or carrier:

You want medical cards sent out to your members on time with their correct names. You want them to invoice the right monthly amount and not get tied up in invoice audits. You want an account management person to respond to you and quickly resolve problems. You do not want issues causing noise among your team. You want excellent execution of the cost containment strategies so you genuinely get costs contained. For example, if they fumble on care navigation, that can cost your plan a lot of money! You don't want to hear about any long claims backlogs with providers calling members for collection on bills that your plan is supposed to pay. You want fast response times for your members when they call customer service with a short time to resolution.

If you have purchased health plans for over three years, you know where this is headed. TPAs have a higher S-factor than the average broker because they do not make more money providing excellent

service; they win no awards. You will probably never talk to an executive at a TPA. They are not incentivized to spend money on process
improvement, measure satisfaction in each customer encounter, or
publish the results of such scoring.

No wonder many employers have concluded there is simply
nothing they can do to improve the situation. "It is what it is," they say.

THERE IS ANOTHER WAY

So obviously, the best scenario is to find a high C-factor broker and
insist they select a high C-factor TPA. It is a fool's errand to change a
broker or TPA unless both have the high C-factor ethos because if
either is terrible, you are in for rough sailing.

If you have over fifty employees, you need to look at either level or
self-funded plans, not just fully-funded plans from the big carriers. If
you are on a fully-funded plan, consider your next steps to get on a
level-funded plan. If you have been on a level-funded plan, consider a
self-funded plan. The self-funded plans can offer the most significant
level of control on the cost containment strategies with the potential to
keep premiums and member out-of-pocket costs in check.

VET YOUR BROKER

Vet your broker to ensure they know what they are doing. You don't
want to be the broker's first level-funded plan recipient. Get a pro who
can tell you which cost containment strategies they recommend. Let
me give you a quick list of ones you should hear about and consider.

Look for methods to:

- Increase the size of the network where your employees live.
- Improve the formulary with the right pharmacy benefits
  manager (PBM) so members have fewer out-of-pocket
  expenses.
- Reduce the cost of expensive procedures beyond merely
  contracted network discounts.

- Offer care navigation to get members significant discounts on major procedures.
- Incentivize members to make good choices.
- Offer better mental health benefits.

Some specifics to ask:

- How will your broker find the best stop-loss carrier, and who will underwrite their claims?
- Will the stop-loss premium underwriters have experience with recommended cost-containment strategies and give credit in the stop-loss premium pricing?
- Will the carrier follow the UW's lead and give credit in pricing?
- How will they select the best TPA?

VET THE TPA OR CARRIER'S ADMINISTRATION

I highly recommend you, or a member of your management team, interview the TPA or the carrier's head of operations. Ask your broker these questions:

What are your key performance indicators (KPI)s for your operations in these areas, and how is your performance against these goals:

- How will they find the best stop-loss carrier, and who will underwrite their claims?
- Will the stop-loss underwriters have experience with the recommended cost-containment strategies and give credit in the premium pricing?
- How will the broker be selecting the best TPA?

It is time to expect more from your broker. If you have one with a high S-factor, make a new plan, Sam! I hope you are now equipped with the questions to ask to help you make the right decision. I am advocating that you take the time to interview the TPA like you would a key employee. Even the best broker has no control over the TPA. TPAs don't take orders from brokers well.

You deserve more than what you are getting, and I hope you are now better armed with how to move forward.

Godspeed!

CHAPTER 12
WE JUST WANT THIS SHIT TO WORK

TOM DILIEGRO

The subject of meaningful health benefits for employees has been bastardized into something expected to be condensed in a sound bite or data point.

———

ANY SUCCESSFUL COMPANY or small business owner will tell you that the key to success is taking care of their employees. For many, taking care of employees means offering them and their families a health and welfare plan. Employers prefer to do this cost-effectively for their companies and to ease the economic burden it places on enrolling employees. Over time, for various reasons, it has become too complicated and expensive. The companies that recognize this take matters into their own hands by offering self-insured plans, cost-sharing programs, or value-based plan design.

As well-intentioned as these efforts are, varying degrees of success are achieved. In most cases, the burden of communicating the new approach falls on uninformed employers. Employees often pay higher out-of-pocket costs via a balance bill or for services and prescription drugs that are no longer covered. No good deed or effort goes unpunished. In response to complaints, the healthcare system inevitably blames employers, providers, and hospitals, with vendors telling employees that their employer offered them a "bad plan" and that they should take it up with their company's human resource (HR) department. So, the system creates an environment where employers need to do something, but when they do, they are punished for their efforts. It's all anyone or any organization can do to keep up and balance, offering something that works that isn't cost-prohibitive or so complex it's unusable.

My personal story is a tale of employer-based benefits and insurance intersecting the way they should. After a lifelong career in warehousing and logistics, my father abruptly found himself back in the job market when his company was sold in the early 1990s. He was in his mid-fifties, had a family to support, and a mortgage to pay. Lucky for our family, the local Star Market warehouse needed someone with his skill set. As a cancer survivor, he would never have considered the job without being offered the core benefit of a group medical plan. He got that, along with group long-term disability and group life insurance, among other offerings.

Then, my father was diagnosed with cancer for the second time. The group medical plan offered by his new company allowed him to receive world-class healthcare without going into debt due to medical expenses. It just worked.

When he got too sick to work, we were able to keep our home because of the long-term disability plan his company offered. It gave my father the dignity to continue providing for his family. Ultimately, when he passed, the life insurance policy allowed my mother to stay in her home, and I was able to further my education.

Star Market provided our family security when life was uncertain. Their employee benefits created a generational legacy for my family by providing what they said they would. We don't shop at Star Market for their weekly deals on eggs and cereal; we shop there because of the kind of company they are and what they did for our family.

This experience ultimately led me to the insurance sector for my career. Unfortunately, modern-day stories of impactful, life-changing benefits are few and far between. This is a shame, as it should be the benchmark of what we expect. Failing to meet this benchmark should be the anomaly, not the norm.

Is it possible for today's modern employer to create that same generational stability available so many years ago? With the high cost of medical care, is it still possible to offer a comprehensive, reliable benefit program to employees when they need it the most?

As Americans, we have been conditioned to think that either someone else (employer, government, or other institution) will pay for our care or we won't seek it. Because of this conditioning, employers must look at what they are offering and how they are paying for it. This is a functional way to care for fellow humans in times of great tragedy or hardship. Charity and goodwill have always been part of how we help pay for those in need, whether the church and guild system from the 1500s or GoFundMe today. Those mechanisms will always have a place in society, and rightfully so. Now, however, I want to look at you, the employer, and ask, what are you doing with your benefits plan, and how are you paying for it?

The original group health plan offered by Montgomery Ward in the early twentieth century was seen as a perk. They employed a strategy to retain their current employees and recruit new talent. Initially, a group health plan was meant to be the equivalent of flex time or a company car—far down on the list of reasons you'd pick one job over another or want to stay at one employer versus moving on to a different one. The difference between then and now is that you, the employer, have been played. You've been played by public policy and the overall healthcare system, who have taken you for granted, believing that you will always be willing and able to pay the bills, whether it be the premium from an insurance carrier or the hospital bill for an employee's care. You see, no one in the business of health-care cares about you. You are the golden goose; you may not realize it, but you have a target on your back. There are many in the industry all too willing to kill the golden goose for their own good. Brokers are after the commission you are worth to them. Vendors and carriers are looking for your service or premium payments. Providers and hospi-tals are counting on you to reduce the aging accounts receivables (AR) they have on their books.

Even if you, as the employer, are paying the bill, it trickles down to your employees. Sustaining a business is about keeping it cash flow positive. So, it is not uncommon when you must pass off healthcare costs to your employees. Sometimes that takes the form of premium hikes which reduces their net pay. Other times, it may mean raising the deductibles so high that you can afford the premium, which means they are paying more out of pocket at the time of care or treatment. Either way, the costs adversely affect both you and them. The intent of a health plan is supposed to be an actual employee benefit, yet employees are picking up a disproportionate amount of the overall costs. This makes it virtually impossible to make a sustainable impact. It is why many Americans technically have insurance but cannot pay for the plan and the care itself. So, I ask again, what are you doing? The answer to that question is that you are likely succumbing to the impact of fear.

Organizations fear not offering a competitive benefits plan that meets current and prospective employees' perceptions of what they feel they should be offered. Employees fear taking a job that doesn't provide "good insurance." The employers I talk to fear organized labor's response to not meeting their expectations and demands. Who benefits from this fear? The same system is extracting so much wealth and resources from private citizens. We are on this feedback loop to maintain the system itself. Those in the healthcare business admit it is flawed but don't know how to manage something different if they stop it. Millions of dollars in electronic medical records (EMR) systems, thousands of jobs in coding and medical billing, and hundreds of carrier service representative positions would be lost. So, the system seems to exist for the system, and employers and employees are asked to pay for it all. But there is a way forward.

We are fortunate to live in a time where everything can be decentralized. We can purchase subscriptions to newspapers and TV programming that deliver content to things we care about, filtering out what we don't. There are meal plans, wardrobes, and single-item packages that can be delivered to our house that meet our individual needs. But in healthcare, employers are still subject to a one size fits all solution offered by a single insurance carrier entity. This puts excessive pressure on the HR manager or chief financial officer (CFO). That individual or committee is being asked to purchase something that a group of people is forced to like, whether you have five or five thousand employees. This is impossible. No wonder so many people hate health insurance.

The industry responds to the negative publicity about the industry with trend reports, surveys, analyses, and benchmarking. Have you asked who funds those reports and surveys? Look at the fine print. It's typically an entity within the industry that has a horse in the product race. I'm not saying they are skewed; I'm not saying they aren't, either.

If many adult Americans were asked to build a "good" health plan, even without industry knowledge, we would know it should be loving, human, and caring—low-cost/no-cost access to good physicians, affordable prescription drugs, and reliable catastrophic financial protections for high-cost and complex conditions, the foundation of any well-functioning health plan.

And here is the fact: a well-functioning plan is easy to build. The solutions are:

- Identify your goals and priorities for the health plan.
- Be willing to implement change.
- Seek well-aligned partners.
- Get access to data.
- Implement a plan based on the data.
- Constantly review and modify.

The problem is finding them and implementing the plans buried under a pile of horse manure that employers must dig through, along with swatting the flies away to maintain it. We see this in everything, the salesperson struggling to get their numbers up or someone struggling with their weight. The resolutions are there, but they are constantly surrounded by a whole bunch of shit. In all cases, a coach, mentor, or friend is needed to help with the shovel or fly swatter to get you where you need to go.

The current benefits model comprises brokers who deliver a product, usually presented on a spreadsheet. They knock on your door, begging to "quote" your insurance, ask for the same things (starting with an employee census), return with information on how great they and their agency are, and then they show you proposals of what they suggest you do moving forward. Let's inject some truth serum into this salesperson. If we did, they would say:

> Hi, I'd like to get the personal information of all your employees to show you a product that will take a top five spot in your spending budget, and your employees will largely hate it. The product is going to cost a huge sum of money. What your employees pay will eat into their after-tax take-home pay, and if something unfortunate happens to them, they will still have to make payments on the expense. The service provider will be frustrated, and despite all the money paid into it, you will have no access to utilization until eleven months later. You then have to take the insurance carriers' word when they say you had a "bad" year, which justifies their increase because your employees didn't adhere to the nuances of our insurance contract.

Would you sign up for that? Based on buying behavior, millions of business owners and HR leaders say yes. For many, buying decisions are based on inertia and fear.

Suppose the wage control provisions during WWII that impacted employer-sponsored healthcare financing never went into place. Without them, the current model would not have been cultivated the way it has. Would group health insurance as we know it still be a thing in the twenty-first century? I admit that I dislike the concept of group-sponsored health insurance. Still, my contempt is less than most, given my experience as a professional in the industry and what I've experienced personally. What I once thought stupid is now something I see that can be beautiful and impactful. I see it as something mutually beneficial to employers, employees, and the communities they exist in. In its purest form, the impact of an excellent company-sponsored health plan for employees is inspiring.

The book *Alcoholics Anonymous* was published in 1939. The writer dedicated a whole chapter to employers. They talk about the human element addressed by employers when outlining their responsibilities to their employees. It states, "Nearly every modern employer feels a moral responsibility for the well-being of his help, and he tries to meet these responsibilities."

The motivation to offer benefits is rooted in the desire to care for employees and others, a decision based on empirical evidence that good benefits lead to greater employee retention and production. Either way, on paper, it should be a simple enough venture in which a product or service would be provided if all parties acted in good faith. The benefits industry has effectively marketed the exact notion that things are simple, and the carriers act in good faith to pay for employees' health and prescription costs. They are very successful in that marketing. Employers bought it hook, line, and sinker.

No one likes being wrong. People have deep-seated beliefs that, in many ways, are core to who we are as individuals. There is pushback when those core beliefs are challenged or proven objectively wrong. The initial response is disbelief. Inevitably the truth sets in.

Similarly, employers have been conditioned to believe their insurance company, local health system, or chain pharmacy has everyone's best interests at heart. I hate to break it to you, but they don't. Recognizing that fact is the first step in creating something for employees that is truly transformational.

Whether it be private equity firms buying out faith-based hospital systems or consolidation among publicly traded "healthcare companies," the industry has turned its back on the paying customer in favor of showcasing returns in quarterly stockholder meetings. It's easy to rail on the industry. In many ways, employers have adopted the same numbers-driven mentality. But you have been lied to. In an effort by brokers and carriers to get lives on the books and by providers to get heads in beds for their benefit, the system, over time, has failed you and your employees.

Recognizing this, a niche subclass within the industry has arisen to address the pressure placed on employers by the hell-th care system. Many within this niche want to be knights in shining armor. From service providers to "advisors," they have reinvented themselves as advocates for employers, riding in to make the rescue. This new industry has many buzzwords and phrases intended to prompt employers to act, disrupt the status quo, or optimize their benefits programs.

Insurance was never meant to be this much at the forefront. Part of the industry's recruiting issues was the perception that it was boring. Newsflash to all the innovators, insurance is supposed to be boring! We need to welcome and embrace boring. We need to market and develop insurance products that, if we do our jobs right, no one will ever have to use. We should be talking about health and quality of life before someone is in the emergency room. Day-to-day care and prescriptions should be accessible and affordable. If they do need to use catastrophic insurance, the products will be there to support them, as promised. We need to replicate the Star Market experience my family had.

Furthermore, employers, for the most part, don't want to run an insurance company. They want to run their organizations to accomplish their mission; employers are not running their businesses to disrupt the insurance business. Far too many niche industry professionals who want to drive change and innovate might be doing so for their own sake, hoping to receive accolades from their peers. Many forget their purpose is to be unknown and off the radar. If their jobs are done right, the employer should receive the credit and attention because they are the entity that desires to change the way business is done. I am qualified to say this because these are my peers, and I have become a part of these niche groups.

The objective of a good benefits advisor is not to be the brightest star in the galaxy but to be the full moon at night. The mission of those of us in the benefits business should be to light the way when things are dark and uncertain. Our products and programs should be prized in a time of need.

There have been countless meetings with employers where we've proposed healthcare options for their employees that they've never heard of—for example, direct primary care, open networks, specialty Rx solutions, and telemedicine, before it was mainstream. These different options are met with skepticism and confusion. Invariably, the "what if" questions start flying; what if someone gets cancer, has premature twins, or is prescribed gene therapy? All those questions are legitimate, and I get where they come from. They are appropriate questions during a benefits conversation when an employer asks about what benefits they will deliver to their team. The motivation, of course, is always financial. Over my career, I've heard these questions many times; now, I respond differently. Before I answer with logistic or technical guidance, I say, "First, we love that person."

What a crazy thing to say in a boardroom setting. When I first mentioned it to an employer who asked me, "what happens when someone gets cancer?" they were caught off guard. It is a sad commentary on the state of the industry when you realize we only talk about terminal cancer in terms of spreadsheets and cost of treatment, with no time considering the human element of the situation. Saying we love the person might seem dismissive, and the first time I said it, I think it was perceived that way. It was as if loving that person and crafting a plan for dealing with the financial impact were mutually exclusive. But are they? We've been thrown together in this cauldron of deadlines, budgets, and short attention spans. The subject of meaningful health benefits for employees has been bastardized into something expected to be condensed in a sound bite or data point. We have traded our souls for a sale, for marginal cost savings on a balance sheet, or a pat on the back for percentage savings in an HR budget.

Many of us in the benefits industry were recruited to it as a quick and easy way to earn a very high income with minimal work. The training consists of obtaining that coveted agent of record letter or finding the gaps in a health plan and exploiting it to save on premiums. The insurance and numbers focus on "winning" because the business trains employers to view the benefits as numbers. Employer clients are treated as prizes we compete for.

People behind those numbers are often forgotten, or their experience navigating healthcare is dismissed because all we have time for is controlling the costs associated with their "condition."

Seeing this led me to question the whole concept of group benefits. I remember thinking how stupid it was that an employer discussed providing their employees health insurance. I mean, if they don't help with car or homeowners' insurance, then why health insurance?

Conservativism questions the idea of benefits being offered by employers. After all, the sole purpose of a for-profit institution is to maximize the wealth of the common stockholder. So how does offering health insurance at the prices companies pay for them lead to that? It doesn't. Therefore, it was something to be managed in a take-it-or-leave-it proposition to employees. "All we have to offer is something that keeps the IRS off our backs, and you're lucky we even do that!" I bought it and couldn't understand any approach to the contrary. If people were robots, it would work.

People are not robots. When a client of mine told me that one of his employees called and thanked him for allowing him to buy his first house and start saving for his kid's college, it validated my belief that we can care about the human experience and the cost. It was the first time I thought *there might be something to this employer-sponsored thing.* The wheels started turning, and I reflected on my personal story. It brought to my attention my past and how my life would have been drastically different without an employer who offered benefits.

When I witness these situations, I'm reminded of my experience as a child. I'm glad Star Market didn't have a broker or an HR department that told employees they would give the minimum to protect the bottom line.

When you think about it, the concept of employer-sponsored benefits is beautiful. It brings together a company and people who benefit from the arrangement when done right. The person being hired has their doors opened to a new community of people and ways of doing things. They are challenged and stretched to their full potential. Everyone benefits from this free exchange of labor. But what's the differentiator between one organization and another? Of course, it is the people and the culture, but what drives the culture? All things equal, pay is a commodity. It's the non-salary benefits that develop the culture. They communicate the culture perhaps better than words and policy books. Benefits are the one thing the employee and their families feel in a time of need, whether medical emergency, health crisis, or death. When an employer is there for an employee, it's a reminder that the employee is part of a tribe—that someone has their back. In thinking about my own experience, knowing my father, we had a hard time paying for groceries or the little extras in life, so there's no way he could have paid for a luxury like long-term disability insurance or life insurance. His employer had our back in a way that no one else could.

After working for a health insurance company, a hospital system, and a third-party administrator, I have realized that not one entity in the industry cares about the end user of their product. Of course, there are people in these organizations that do, but carriers count premium dollars, health systems count reimbursement dollars, and all other entities count "lives" under contract.

The broker/consultant/agent/adviser must care. In a way, they need to act as a kind of employer mind reader, independently supervising plan operations. They exist to fulfill your vision. To do so, you need to know and share what that vision is.

CHAPTER 13
HINDSIGHT IS 20/20: LITERALLY

RACHEL MINER

It's important to know why our system is in its current shape because costs will not decrease; this isn't a phase.

───────

IMAGINE for a second that you and I take our families on vacation. Imagine that we do not know the price of these vacations before taking the trip. We go to the same resort, stay for the same duration, eat at the same restaurants, and then when the final bill arrives, I pay with my Visa, and you pay with an American Express, and our charges differ by more than $10,000. Would you find it ludicrous, or would you pay it and think nothing of it? Would you ask for an itemized bill to examine where the discrepancies lie?

If this scenario seems far-fetched, imagine another where we would consume something before knowing the price. Let me be the first to welcome you to the United States healthcare system. If you want to know how prices are determined, you can't because that's proprietary knowledge. Healthcare and health insurance are purposefully confusing you to maximize revenues for hospitals, carriers, and pharmacy benefit managers. This has put our country in a tough spot.

It's essential to understand how we got into this healthcare crisis.

It's also important to know that you have power as a consumer and an employer. You're probably sick of hearing about health insurance and paying outrageous premiums. I don't blame you. Many people did not question the cost of health insurance and healthcare until the Patient Protection and Affordable Care Act (PPACA, aka ACA) healthcare reform law was enacted in March 2010 and incrementally phased in since. The law had three primary goals. The first goal was to make healthcare more affordable for those falling between 100 and 400 percent of the federal poverty level. The second goal of PPACA was to support any medical innovations that could help lower the cost of healthcare. The third goal was to expand Medicaid coverage to cover adults with incomes 138 percent and below the federal poverty level.

Let's consider how PPACA has performed on these objectives. Ultimately, whether the ACA has made healthcare more affordable is a subjective call because it shifted the cost liability from one group of individuals to another. For most lower-income individuals, total spending (meaning deductible + premium costs) has fallen because of the coverage and subsidies they've gotten under the ACA in the individual marketplace. For these people, PPACA accomplished its goal and likely changed lives. However, for most higher-income individuals (especially those not eligible for subsidies), the cost of premiums and out-of-pocket expenses has dramatically increased. Those who do not get coverage on the individual open market but through an employer-sponsored health plan and higher-income individuals have seen similar expense increases. Over 49 percent of all covered under health insurance have an employer-sponsored plan; it's fair to say that many people have seen increases in total spending since 2010.

Before PPACA, some people likely thought of health insurance as an endless pool of money to pull from; at least, I know I did when my deductible was only $500.00. According to the Kaiser Family Foundation, in 2010, the average individual deductible on a PPO plan for single coverage was $675. Deductibles in 2020, merely a decade later, have risen to $1,204. There is a starker difference for High Deductible Health Plans (HDHPs), with single coverage deductibles in 2020 averaging $2,303 with premium contributions averaging $7,470 for individual-only coverage. Since 2010, the cost of premiums has increased by

55 percent. This is more than two times the wage increases in that same time frame! It's also important to note that health insurance company stocks have been thriving during this period.

The second goal of PPACA was to encourage healthcare innovations, primarily payment and delivery models. Since 2014, there has been an increased focus on healthcare IT and a spotlight on population management. Over the past decade, several other innovations have come about inadvertently due to the rising cost of care. Such innovations include healthcare concierge apps that can guide consumers to the right place at the right time to get the appropriate care they need, pharmacogenomics (where an individual's genetic makeup is analyzed to see how effective a therapeutic drug can be for them) and virtual care. This goal of PPACA can only be realized if these innovations are used and communicated with employees and members.

The last goal of PPACA was to expand Medicaid, and it has proven to be a challenge, with twelve states strongly refusing to participate. For some states, it has ruined state budgets, overrun hospitals, and expanded Medicaid to many non-disabled adults who don't need the program. States that have participated are enrolling significantly more people than they initially projected (well over double), which has resulted in millions - even billions of dollars - that have fallen on the shoulders of taxpayers like you, me, and your employees.

Although PPACA had three main objectives, several other additions to the law were also made.

- Dependents can stay on their parent's medical insurance until they are twenty-six years old.
- There can be no discrimination against a person due to a pre-existing condition.
- Instead of the historical one to two-million dollar limit on what insurance would pay, the maximum lifetime benefit is now unlimited.

The last part is the most important because it opened the floodgates to why our costs in healthcare have gotten so out of control. When these costs started getting too high, carriers began to suggest plan design changes to help employers (remember, they make up half of the insured) with the rising costs. Their fix was high-deductible health plans. These plans had significantly lower premiums and encouraged employees to partake in cost-sharing for health insurance spending. The benefit to an employee was that they could participate in Health Savings Accounts. This money could go into a bank account tax-free, grow tax-free, and not be taxed when used on qualified medical expenses. While the cost shifting did open employees' eyes to the actual cost of healthcare services, since it is not first-dollar coverage, it also made many people refrain from accessing the care they needed or refuse to pay their cost-sharing portion because they couldn't afford it.

My love/hate relationship with our healthcare system began in 2013, the year my son was born. This was when I learned that the term "sick care" is a more accurate description of our present healthcare system. It is over-testing and prolonged treatments because they are far more lucrative for hospitals than curing. Hospital-owned physicians maximize revenue by referring into their facilities and reactive versus proactive care. What opened the door for this? PPACA's unlimited life-time maximum.

My son, Jackson, was always sick when he was two years old. He vomited daily for over a month, had a fever of 104 intermittently, and lost eight pounds. I went to our pediatrician, who was affiliated with our local hospital system, almost every day for a month straight. Jackson was tested for Kawasaki Disease, Reyes Syndrome, Cystic Fibrosis, and a million other things for which he wasn't showing symptoms. Ultimately, he landed in the hospital and spent seven days there. During his stay, I talked to the doctors daily and told them what I had researched and what I thought could be wrong with him. One condescending doctor asked me where I received my medical degree. At nine months pregnant with my third child and sleeping in a hospital bed with a seriously ill child, it probably wasn't the wisest comment for the doctor to make (thanks, Dr. Joe, you asshole). From the first day we were in the hospital, I asked if he could have mononu-cleosis (commonly referred to as mono.) The doctors told me it was unlikely and didn't test him for it until five days after we arrived. He tested *positive*. Our insurance was billed $96,000 for that hospital stay. The mono test was only $59.

My son endured test after test, and no one advocated for him except me. I learned that I had to ask questions about the things that didn't make sense in healthcare. I had to question doctors' opinions and the necessity of tests. I had to play an active role in his care and not simply follow their directions or advice.

It's important to know why our system is in its current shape because costs will not decrease; this isn't a phase. Knowing there are things they can do to lower the cost of medical procedures and prescriptions for your employees and their families makes a significant impact. It could be the difference between being able to afford a life-saving medication or not.

CHAPTER 14
KYP

DR. MADELINE SMITH

The first step to navigating American healthcare is learning who's playing the game with you and what everyone's role is.

———

BEING MARRIED to a sports aficionado and a mom to three boys who are all convinced they will play in the NFL (and who think the NBA is a realistic backup plan), I've learned things without even trying (or wanting to sometimes). Over the last month, one sports concept has been ringing loudly through my head: KYP. Know Your Personnel.

I won't do justice to my husband's typical soliloquy to our oldest son, but essentially, it was originally a football term that is a reminder that you need to know who's on the field, their skills, and what their role is in that play. When you think about the art of football or sports in general, any modicum of success requires communication, integration, planning, awareness, and elite performance levels.

Many watch sports as an escape or a pastime (or perhaps to win back the money they lost during last week's game). Either way, most don't watch it to admire the complex operations involved taking place behind the scenes. We don't watch it to critique the billions of dollars that go into every week's schedule and the months of offseason planning and preparation (although operations nerds with backgrounds in event planning like myself probably do). In a bizarre way, the health-care and health insurance world are viewed similarly.

KYP isn't the only part of football we can and should learn from in this business, yet it seems to be the most relevant. The ecosystem around every health plan comprises many moving parts. I've seen it portrayed as a wheel, with the employer (plan sponsor) as the hub. Legally, this is correct but operationally, not so much. It's more akin to an amoeba-shaped org chart with appendages in multiple places, all mostly unaware of the others. It rarely works the way it's supposed to.

What stood out to me when I first entered the industry was how it seemed no one knew their role. What's more, no one knew anyone else's role! So, without clearly defined roles and responsibilities, many vendors, multiple income streams (many of which are hidden), and a constantly changing healthcare market, we have a recipe for disaster. What an employer does with their health plan is up to them, but, we *can* make those decisions easier and more efficient if all parties involved know everyone's roles and responsibilities.

I often joke that no one reads the terms and conditions of being an employer who's offering a group health plan. You might say it is because there is a published terms and conditions document some-where. In reality, there are numerous. Depending on various character-istics of their company or health plan, employers may have to adhere to the terms of numerous regulations like ERISA and ACA. There are other guiding documents and policies that must be adhered to such as service contracts, business associate agreements, network contracts, stop-loss policies, etc.

Let's break down who's who within the group health plan ecosystem and what the rules of engagement are. I vacillate between putting members/employees or the employer first on this list of Who's Who. We can probably agree I tied them for first place in the order of importance. You wouldn't be offering a health plan, nor would you have a business if it wasn't for your employees. Conversely, they wouldn't have group benefits or a job if it wasn't for you. In its purest form, it should be a symbiotic relationship.

EMPLOYEES (AND THEIR DEPENDENTS)

Despite what you (or they) may think, employees have a role and responsibilities within the health plan ecosystem. Some of their impact is based on demographic information, while others are based on consumer behavior. Let's unpack this a little. First, we've established that the cost of your health plan is tied to its underwritten risk—what underwriters and carriers believe the cost to insure your employee population is. There are many nuances to underwriting, many of which are discussed in this book, which we cannot adequately outline here. Demographic information is one element that many employers do not realize has an impact. The average age of your employee population and the ratio of males to females impacts your overall cost of risk. So does the geographic location of your employees. There is an argument to be made for hiring practices, remembering to look to fill the positions with candidates with favorable demographic features. Favorable in this case is not suggesting superiority or risk cost assumptions (although this author personally believes women run the world). On the other side of the argument are those who believe positions should be filled by the right individual with the right experience, and expertise, regardless of their demographic features that affect the overall cost of the group's risk. Demographics are somewhat immovable for the purpose of underwriting. Without altering or crafting a hiring strategy with this in mind, the demographic data for your employee population will be what it will be.

The next way your employees impact the cost of your group health plan is their consumer behavior. While difficult and sensitive, this is not inflexible. It is neither your right nor responsibility to control how your employees access and use healthcare.

Considering you are footing at least a portion of the bill it makes sense that you could do certain things to influence this access and use. There are countless examples, but let's analyze a few diverse ones here:

Emergency room visits: These visits are killers for all plans. I must acknowledge there are some scenarios when nothing makes sense except going to the ER. It's also very common that people go to the ER because they are unsure where else to go, or if the situation is of an unknown cause, they would end up there anyway. This is where education and plan design can intersect to serve everyone. Whether you like it or not, you are in the benefits business. Since you offer it, you may as well make sure it's being utilized as intended. Sharing information with employees and their families about what constitutes an emergency (heart attack/stroke symptoms, severe injuries, etc.) and what doesn't (needing a prescription refill, non-allergy rashes, sore throat, pink eye, etc.) can be a great place to start. Once you've done that (repeatedly and consistently throughout the plan year, not just once at enrollment), that's where benefit design comes in. How have you made alternatives to ER visits accessible and affordable? Do you offer virtual care/telemedicine? Is it affordable or even free to use? Do you have a lower copay for urgent care than you do for ER? Do you offer low or no copays for primary care visits?

Maternity care/birthing centers: Access to quality and affordable maternity and prenatal care throughout a member's pregnancy is vital to having a sustainable health plan. Without it, many will forego adequate care only to face complications or issues late in their pregnancy or delivery. Another little-known fact is that birthing centers and non-traditional methods of maternity care and delivery offer lower costs and higher-quality experiences with lower risks. Some plans do not even cover birthing centers or doulas, let alone incentivize them. An emerging awareness of this leads some plans to reduce patient costs when they utilize doulas or birthing centers instead of traditional hospital settings for delivery.

Specialty & high-cost Rx: This is one element of modern-day health care that many of us are all too familiar with, whether because of personal experience or news stories. In my experience on the risk side of this, three situations generally describe specialty and high-cost Rx. The first is the case where the drug prescribed is for a clinically vital, life-sustaining reason, and that particular brand is the most appropriate solution based on that specific patient. The second is the case where the drug prescribed is for a clinically vital, life-sustaining reason, but multiple brands would work. The particular brand is being utilized because either the doctor is receiving incentives to promote it or the formulary is geared toward maximizing rebate dollars without regard for cost to the patient or the health plan. The third is the case of a lifestyle drug that exists to improve a patient's quality of life rather than cure an illness or reduce pain. It is not my place (or a health plan's) to say what meds a member should or shouldn't get. But, it's worth putting a program in place that supports HOW members access these expensive medications, especially when there are cost-effective ways to do so. Putting in a specialty Rx program can mitigate some of your highest severity plan expenses and ensure your employees and their dependents are getting the medications they need. Once you have a program like this, do employees go there first to discover the best path forward to fill their expensive prescriptions, or do they do what they've always done?

Chronic condition maintenance: This is analyzed through both the medical and pharmacy programs. Essentially, it looks at whether your employees and their dependents with chronic conditions adhere to their required protocols (i.e., regular required visits, filling and taking chronic maintenance medications, getting regularly scheduled blood draws, etc.). High member adherence to these translates to better long-term performance of your health plan. If you're interested, your advisor can probably get you reports on how your members are doing with this (de-identified, of course). You can then be empowered to do something with your data and incentivize or reward adherence!

On one hand, it is important that your employees don't see their health plan as simply a credit card. On the other, it is vital that your plan is designed with access, efficiency, and affordability at the core. How members utilize the health plan and navigate the specialized programs you've put in place will affect the cost of your plan (much like demographics do).

Your employees and dependents have a role in this even though they do not realize it. The most effective strategy you can employ is to design a plan that gives them easily accessible, affordable programs. Then, open dialogue within the company about your vision for the health plan and what role they can play. I would encourage this to be an empowering conversation rather than a punitive one.

EMPLOYERS & PLAN SPONSORS

I'm struggling with finding the words to sugarcoat this, so I will say it: the buck stops with you. Ultimately, the majority of the responsibility for having a compliant, sustainable health plan is on you. I'm not saying it's fair; it is just what it is. Because most employers offer a health plan and don't intend to become health insurance compliance experts, it is common for employers to hire help. This involves selecting a broker or hiring a third-party administrator or pharmacy benefit manager. But that's how you need to look at it - they are here to represent YOU and help you fulfill your obligation. That's very different than seeing their role to sell you products or broker your rates with the carrier. Would you select a different broker if you look at it from that perspective? Would you manage the meetings differently? Would you select your vendors using a different approach? Who would drive the benefits initiative?

The selection of brokers and vendors is your first responsibility as an employer. Next comes plan design. You design a compliant, efficient plan design that aligns with your vision. Again, you can do this alone and tell your broker or consultant what you want to do, or you can have your broker design it with your input. Ultimately, it's your responsibility.

Ongoing plan management and compliance is your next responsibility. This is a broad, far-reaching responsibility that includes report review, benchmark analysis, employee communication, adherence to service agreements, and compliance with applicable contracts. If you are self-funded, when a provider appeals, it's your responsibility to review and respond to the appeal. You can either do this yourself or hire your third-party administrator (TPA). It is your job to ensure your plan is administered according to your plan document. You hire a third-party administrator to administer the plan, but it is your job to ensure they do what you've hired them to do. For example, if your plan requires prior authorization for certain procedures, it is your job to ensure the administrator is facilitating that. If you don't, your carrier may likely deny the claim, and then you will discover too late that the plan is being administered poorly. If your plan excludes or limits specialty medication, your responsibility is to make sure your pharmacy benefit manager and TPA are administering accordingly. When you evaluate renewal options, it's your responsibility to make sure you are selecting an option that covers what you are looking for, rather than being surprised six months later that you left yourself exposed in a particular area.

Now more than ever, you probably realize why the partners you surround yourself with are more important than you may have known. Selecting these partners cannot be based on how pretty and glossy their reports are or how well they sell themselves. You need to find the partners you want in the trenches with you. Whether they are simply executing your wishes or doing the research and crafting the offering, they are more than merely "a vendor."

THIRD-PARTY ADMINISTRATORS (TPA)

You might think that my outline of the roles and responsibilities of a third-party administrator will be extensive. It is not. The roles and responsibilities of a TPA are whatever the administrative service agreement (ASA) you signed says they are. They are strictly an administrator of the plan you and your broker design and build. They have a few key responsibilities that should be outlined in the ASA. These include adjudicating claims according to your plan document, processing your payment of claims, providing customer service support for your members, verifying eligibility and benefits to providers who call, providing ID cards and necessary plan documentation, etc.

I have worked with and for countless TPAs over the years, so you can trust me when I say you will be disappointed if you count on your TPA to design your plan, educate your employees, and be proactive in creating new and creative strategies for cost containment and plan performance. I'm not saying they aren't capable of it or that no TPAs do it. I'm simply saying they aren't contracted to do so in most cases, and that is not what you are paying them for. Your most effective approach would be to find a TPA who has experience administering a plan with provisions like yours, has a proven record of accurate, timely claims processing, expert-level knowledge of stop-loss and compliance-related issues, high-quality customer service, and a robust, experienced staff to support you and your employees. If you find the right partner, make sure you (and/or your broker) explicitly articulate what you expect of them and ensure those expectations are memorialized in your signed agreement. Then, stay in constant communication with them, your broker, your stop-loss carrier, and your members to ensure they deliver.

PHARMACY BENEFIT MANAGERS (PBM)

There is so much to say about the role and responsibilities of PBMs that an entire book could be written on it, although it would be even more controversial than this one. To explain more than confuse, I will say that the role of your PBM should be similar to that of a TPA. Technically, a PBM is the interface between drug companies and insurers (whether fully insured carriers or self-funded plan sponsors). They *should* work to lower plan and member costs for medication. Unfortunately, like many aspects of modern-day healthcare and insurance, it has become a highly corrupted industry. Not all PBMs are corrupt; some do an incredible job of representing their clients, negotiating aggressive discounts on medication without pocketing the savings, providing nationwide access to pharmacies, and providing excellent customer service. When selecting a PBM, those are the elements you should look for. These should also be the metrics by which you measure and evaluate the effectiveness of your current PBM.

STOP-LOSS CARRIERS

Stop-loss is technically catastrophic coverage. It is what protects you from the above-expected high-frequency claims or high-severity claims. It is the insurance that limits your liability above and beyond what you can control with effective risk management. The carrier has responsibilities, but to discern them, you must see the actual protection as just that: protection for the elements of risk you can't control.

The carrier is responsible for underwriting your plan and providing you with rates. They are responsible for covering any claims you file with them that meet the policy terms. They are responsible for communicating with you, your broker, your administrator, and anyone else representing you. They are responsible for complying with state, federal laws and regulations and are legally authorized to issue policies in your locale.

When selecting your carrier, I cannot stress enough that you should look for more than simply rates. As a novice in the industry, I analyzed carriers exclusively by who offered the best coverage at the cheapest rate. As I gained more experience and navigated unforeseen situations, I learned the invaluable benefit of selecting a carrier you revere as a partner. These carriers will work collaboratively with you, your broker, and TPA. They will value your creative strategies and perhaps even offer them discounts on your premium. They will respond to and pay your claims accurately and quickly. They will issue fair renewals, but even more important, they will explain how they came to their rating. When things happen that fall in grey areas (and they will), they will not always interpret those one-off situations in a way that protects them from paying claims.

PROVIDER NETWORK

I've debated whether they deserve their unique section. On one hand, it's difficult and partially inaccurate to lump all provider networks into one category. But it's essential for you to know what your provider network isn't. They are not your only path to adequate healthcare. They are also not all in existence to make healthcare cheaper using the discounts they offer. Some will do this and will do it exquisitely. Others will create the illusion of savings while dramatically increasing your costs. If you utilize a network, read your network access or service agreement. No matter what you feel, that agreement will outline their responsibilities. You may be surprised if you read the fine print. When evaluating or managing your provider network, look for adequate access to care, provider credentialing, ability to audit claims when necessary, reporting functionality, compliance, and reasonable terms and costs.

Some other entities and vendors play a role in your plan, but they are minor actors compared to the ones covered here. You'll notice brokers and consultants do not have their own section here. This is because I feel like I gave them adequate attention in Chapter 9. The first step to navigating American healthcare is learning who's playing the game with you and what everyone's role is.

Knowing your roles and responsibilities and the other players involved with your health plan, you should feel less like you're trapped in Abbott and Costello's "Who's On First" and ready to build or improve on a sustainable benefits strategy.

CHAPTER 15
20 YEARS OF SELLING: A DRUG DEALIN' DITTY

RACHEL STRAUSS

It's up to those buying the benefits to not only demand change but also facilitate those changes until they become the new norm.

———

SOMETHING intriguing about this book's title had me clamoring to have a voice inside its pages. Because you, dear reader, are here for a reason. Maybe, the reason is simply discovering the actual "MoFos" pulling the strings in healthcare, or you're ready to face the legalized larceny this book is uncovering. And, like any good drama, there's a plot twist. Because at the heart of the system, the intent is to provide best-in-class benefits. But instead, if the system has done one thing, it has made money for so many corporations while decreasing the care patients receive. And who's paying the largest percentage of this bill? You, as American employers.

I work in a specialized segment of healthcare: pharmacy benefits. Those two words are simple enough to translate, but in reality, it is an endless rabbit hole that can cause even the most trained consultant to get dizzy going down its dark path. With nearly twenty-one years in this industry, I'm amazed by the twists and turns within pharmacy benefit management (PBM).

What is truly remarkable about the PBM industry is that there are ways to fix the problems. It's up to those buying the benefits to not only demand change but also facilitate those changes until they become the new norm. But first, let's review what the PBM industry is supposed to be about.

I know a healthcare consultant who has always equated the many facets of healthcare to ice cream shops (I happen to be married to him).[1] When you buy fully insured benefits from the large carriers, he says it's like going to Baskin Robbins. Yes, they offer a variety of flavors (thirty-one, to be exact). But what's in the tub is all you can get. When you enter the world of self-funding, it's like walking into Marble Slab, where you pick every single ingredient. And, if this book is read carefully, you will understand not only the power of choosing those "mix-ins" but how to ensure the flavors meld well together.

In my field, where the PBMs live, our role was supposed to be simple: manage a network of pharmacies, negotiate discounts, and build clinical formularies (what drugs are covered and how) that are safe for patients while being cognizant of the bottom line for both patient and end-payer (whether employer or carrier). It's interesting how little people know about our industry, especially because ninety-five percent of every prescription in the country annually is processed through a PBM versus the five percent that is cash pay.[2] If you ask any insured American who their healthcare coverage is, they will know the name on their card. But if you ask them who pays for their prescriptions, they likely will have no idea.

In recent years, America's plan sponsors and employers have taken notice of their pharmacy benefits. This was primarily due to the extreme cost trend blamed on pharmaceutical advancements; their hefty prices were passed on to employers.

When you start to scratch the surface, there are so many areas for scrutiny, and Washington finally seems to be catching on. It's no wonder the medications that are increasing in popularity are also the ones airing several commercials an hour on TV. It's worth considering why some pharmacy chains (the ones that are household names) are suddenly no longer part of some of the largest national healthcare insurers. Why are you seeing a medication advertised as a $4 generic at

Walmart, show up on your top drug report costing $50 per script? These are questions that PBMs must answer. Here is where our legal larceny drama series segues into the next adventure: how some PBMs conduct business like the cartels.[3]

For every answer we discover, we uncover new questions in our industry. Some say it's an industry of smoke and mirrors; others say PBMs are the main reason for cost increase across the board. For more than two decades, I have been an employee of a "boutique" PBM rather than one of the three largest. The "boutique" segment relies on transparency, honesty, and a true mission to do what's right for all parties involved—the reason PBMs was started to begin with.

I will share what eye-opening experiences I encountered early in my career; hopefully, this provides some awareness that employers can shape into strategy as they build out plans.

Remember early on, when I shared my husband's example of how self-funding is like choosing your adventure in ice cream with your mix-ins? Well, no matter how "best in class" (or delicious, in this example), your partners may be on their own—it's up to you to ensure everyone works together as you build a health plan. When someone chooses us as their PBM partner, they must direct us on whom we work with. Sometimes it's with big carrier-owned *third-party* administrators (TPAs). More often, it's with boutique TPAs. But either way–as a vendor, it can feel like an arranged marriage. Without someone nurturing the relationship—assuring that all of us understand our role, so we aren't silos doing just our own thing—it is impossible to "fall in love."

For example, many medications are often significantly more expensive when you purchase them within a hospital setting. Only a PBM will know this with access to the proper pricing methodology. However, members in the hospital will be handled financially through the TPA's clinical management process. If the TPA never consults the PBM during their pre-certification process, they may approve a higher-cost medication to be administered through the hospital. Both member and plan sponsors suffer while the hospitals earn unnecessary revenue. This can be avoided by assuring your partners work together even outside the scope of their services.

And then there's the entire model of the PBM you work with. Chapters can exist on this topic alone, but I'll give the highlights in a mission of brevity. The entire basis of the model will depend on your PBM's declaration of how they get paid. Again, I am employed by a PBM and depend on one for my livelihood, so it is no surprise that I believe PBMs have a purpose and should get paid properly to do the intended job. However, the mystery remains for so many PBMs: *How do the PBMs earn revenue?*

It's a simple enough question, yet if you're looking for a simple answer, you will find yourself navigating a tunnel with no light in sight. For many (many) years, PBMs charged no administrative fees. That's right—you could have a contract for thousands of employees for a sizeable self-funded plan with clearly disclosed administrative fees for *every* line of coverage except Rx (medical, dental, vision, ancillary, etc.). When it came to the pharmacy portion, the most frequently used by members as so many take at least one prescription per month, there was a $0 fee on your admin statement. Or even better, what we see in our world with the carrier-owned PBM model is a *credit* to have their RX program! I recently bid against a carrier-owned PBM where the group had a $30 PEPM (per employee per month) admin fee credit built into their medical fee, making it nearly impossible for another carrier to seem competitive.

Once we peeled back the layers and looked to find where this was coming from, we discovered the incumbent PBM was marking up the spread on the prescriptions the members used by nearly 20 percent to accommodate the credit on the other side. This means that for every drug a member got from the pharmacy, the bill was 20 percent more than the PBM was reimbursing the pharmacy. And–this was just what we found on competitor analysis. It's nearly impossible with rebate contracts, undisclosed margins, and other tricks of the trade, to iden-tify all the areas for profit for a PBM. The key you want to look for, if you want to try to get to the bottom of it, is to look for transparency and a PBM being honest with where their revenue sources come from.

So, to simplify such a difficult part of what was designed to be complex, be sure any partner you choose as a vendor of benefits to your employees is accountable for what they do and is compensated for performing as such. It really can be controlled!

---

1. Self-Funding 31 Flavors – Levi Strauss, Assured Partners Houston
2. The Driver Dictating Prescription Drug Benefits: PBMs Explained
3. PBM Monopoly The Nation's Largest Legal Cartels

CHAPTER 16

YOU ONLY KNOW WHAT YOU KNOW

ERIKA ENSIGN

Find the folks who will stand in the damn ring and fight alongside you and your employees!

———

SO, what do you do to know more, do more, and make an impact on your organization that *you* desire? Let's keep things simple for now Get honest with yourself—like *real fucking honest!*

Ask yourself these questions within the context of your employee benefits plan:

- What do I want?
- What do I know?
- What can I do?

To get from where you are to where you want to go, you must start by being honest. Look, no one is here to judge or condemn you (mainly because *none* of us have it all figured out). Still, if we can't effectively get to the starting point, there is no way in hell that we will ever be able to get to the finish line.

WHAT DO I WANT?

This question may sound simple, but the answers are limitless and sometimes quite hard to answer or articulate effectively. Here are some basic questions to ask yourself, "What do I want?"

Why do you provide your employees insurance benefits? What was your goal when you first offered those benefits? What did you want to accomplish by investing in health benefits? What do you want your employees to experience and understand about their benefits? Do they think they are actually "benefiting" from them? What is *their* perspective? In a world where perception is quite honestly reality, what is your employees' reality?

Let's move from your employees to you for a second. Understand that whatever you initially had in mind when you first offered employees benefits quite possibly has changed over the years. Is what you want now completely different from what you wanted back then? Have you thought about it recently? If you are like most folks, chances are, you have succumbed to what I like to call "habitual benefits" does this sound familiar?

Maybe you've found yourself thinking:

We have always had these plans and moved carriers a few times — that was a racket. Our broker shops it yearly, and we have all that is available. It is what it is.

What if you could change the narrative? What if you could use your employee benefits program as a vehicle to *benefit* your employees for things like:

- attraction
- retention
- sustainability of cost
- adequate access to care
- Fill in the blank here with what you want it to do for you and your employees.

WHAT DO I KNOW?

Ok, you have what you want; let's get even more honest. Dare I say vulnerable, and ask yourself: *What do I actually know?* Or *what do I believe I know?* If you *think* you have it all figured out, know what to do, and how to do it, yet you are still running into a brick wall, then something is wrong with your formula, and you do *not* know everything. The good news is *no one*, I repeat, *no one* knows it all, nor can they do it all by themselves, so stop lying to yourself. If what you want is not your current reality, then you need some help. Welcome to the fucking club—the human club. To get from where you are to where you want to go, you must admit where you are (good, bad, and ugly) to know where you are starting from.

And let me say this, being honest by allowing yourself to be vulnerable enough to admit where you are in this journey is the first step to getting what/where you want to go. It must be measurable—I mean, don't you want to look back and reflect on how far you have come? Well, then, you must know where your starting point is. More good news: if your answer is, "I have no clue where I am," then know that you are in more company than you may realize. Let me help you out here; you run a business that, chances are, has *zero* to do with insurance in any capacity (health or commercial), so understandably, you may know next to nothing or nothing at all! So here we go; you know *nothing*. We have a starting point, folks; now let's go to the next question.

WHAT CAN I DO?

You may have heard the expression, "Find your tribe." Well, this expression holds even in this industry. If you are at this point and have been honest with yourself, you have realized you can't do it alone and shouldn't. This industry took decades to become the monster it is today—one of the most hated and misunderstood industries. Don't believe me? Ask anyone not in this business if they like insurance (insurance of any kind).

I would even venture to say that most people who do this for a living hate it. As it turns out, there is still a high level of "hidden" information that they also don't understand. But when you get down to the basics of it all, what we want isn't necessarily "insurance" it is the basic want/need for adequate access to healthcare. Excuse the hell out of us for *also* wanting it to be for a reasonable, affordable, and sustainable cost! I mean, who do we think we are asking for some basic shit like access to doctors, hospitals, and medication for a reasonable cost? Ok, so you know what you want, you know what you know (or what you don't), so what do you do? How do you find the people who can help you? Start asking the simple questions, the *whys & hows*: "Why are our plans like this?" "How did the carrier come up with these rates?" "Why are these claims paid at this cost?" "How can you help us?" If you are not getting a straight answer, they either don't know or are intentionally not telling you. If it's the latter, ask why again.

The more you ask, the clearer picture you will gain of whom has your organization as a priority vs. the carrier/vendor. Where does the loyalty lie? How are your partners genuinely helping you? *Spreadshitting* once a year is *not* a partnership. For those that aren't familiar- "spreadshitting" is when a consultant or partner does not have much to offer, so they try to hide it on a big-ass spreadsheet to impress/distract you. *If* you want a true partner, there is no magic formula, nor is there a proprietary carrier/coverage—it's the *action* behind your program that is built. I am sure that by now, many people have presented ideas to help your company. Ideas are fantastic, but if you do not have people in the seats managing and steering those ideas into action, those fantastic ideas are, well, just ideas.

A plan without execution, monitoring, and adjustments will always be just a "pipe dream." Grandiose plans are often created and sold to manifest into nothing more than frustrations and disappointments.

Find the folks who will stand in the damn ring and *fight* alongside you and your employees! If you have created a program for a specific reason, the vendors and carriers who make up this program will only be as great as the accountability they are held to. Will things be perfect? No–we are all humans and make mistakes. Years ago, a client told me: "Erika, it's ok when mistakes are made; that is certain to happen. What's important is the action taken to resolve the mistake because humans don't have it all figured out, and we will never do it perfectly." What we can do is constantly work to find ways to make it better. It's ok to hold your partners accountable; it's ok to question a bill from a hospital; it's ok to ask the cash price for medication; it's ok not to use your health insurance plan; it's ok to challenge the system because this is the *only* way we are *ever* going to get out from underneath this racket.

Moving your plan from fully insured to self-funded is *great*, but what are you doing with the data you now have access to? Simply being self-funded isn't enough. What are you doing with the data, the claims, and how are you helping to stabilize costs, even lower them? What can be done? You won't know if you don't ask questions. My advice for you is the same advice I once got from a good friend and colleague in the business:

> *As you ask more questions, you may start questioning your sanity–you may even think the people you are asking (providers, pharmacies, and vendors) think you're crazy for asking questions. Just know right before you believe you are insane, the truth is right around the corner, so keep pushing, keep asking.*

CHAPTER 17
INERTIA IS A BITCH

DR. MADELINE SMITH

Change is hard. Even when it's right.

———

IT NEVER CEASES to amaze me how many employers make terrible decisions that cost them tens or sometimes hundreds of thousands of dollars for one simple reason—inertia.

Miriam Webster's Dictionary defines inertia as:

"A property of matter by which it continues in its existing state of rest or uniform motion in a straight line unless that state is changed by an external force."

In my humble opinion, that is the most accurate description of what's happening within employer-sponsored health plans. We could take a long walk through history and analyze how much has changed within health plans sponsored by employers, exclusively driven by external forces. Instead, we'll acknowledge the most recent influences.

The Affordable Care Act (ACA) has significant Employer Shared Responsibility provisions. It's often called the employer mandate or the "pay or play provisions." It dramatically changed the way applicable large employers offered coverage to their employees.

Some guidelines address what employers must do and not do,

while other provisions within the ACA articulate what benefits must be offered or how they must be designed. There are many rules, provisions, and guidelines required by group health plans, many of which are not understood or even known by employers. To address this, some carriers changed plan designs, or advisors helped employers restructure their offerings or contributions.

New disclosure regulations have recently changed how fees are disclosed to employer groups. The No Surprises Act aimed to protect individuals from surprise bills, but unsuspecting employers and vendors faced new and increasing responsibilities.

These are regulatory stimuli. Not all impactful changes prompted by external forces are triggered by regulation. Some are simply reactions to force majeure.

A recent example of this (although perhaps somewhat traumatic to discuss) is COVID. COVID changed not only health plans and coverage but many aspects of human resources. No one had a choice but to react and respond to the crisis for corporate survival.

Whether prompted by regulation or pandemics no one saw coming, inertia wasn't an option. Forced change isn't always bad, and in the way it helps us combat inertia, it serves us well. Many of us industry professionals watched groups now forced to make unwanted changes in order to prevent layoffs.

Let's examine a few ways inertia hurts us:

- keeping the same unhelpful broker
- renewing with the same carrier year over year and facing double-digit increases
- insisting on the same network every year, despite watching dollars flying out the window
- staying fully insured and essentially giving the carrier free money when self-funding would make the most sense for your group

I get it. It's easier—all of it. Let's look at it from a different perspective, though. Finding a new broker is hard; bankrolling an ineffective broker is hard. Pick your hard.

Going through a rigorous Request for Proposal (RFP) is hard; swallowing undeserved double-digit increases every year is hard. Pick your hard.

Changing networks is hard; paying your current network for access *and* watching how much you are paying in claims is hard. Pick your hard.

Being self-funded is hard; staying fully insured and giving the carrier free money is hard. Pick your hard.

Getting HR on board with a new strategy is hard; hearing HR struggle with budget or recruiting obstacles is hard. Pick your hard.

Having employees support a change is hard; having employees complain about how bad their benefits are, no matter what you put in place, is hard. Pick your hard.

If you are reading this, you likely either built a business (or many) or are running one today. This list of what you deal with that's "hard" would probably be comical if it wasn't your reality.

If you are making a conscious choice to relish in the inertia, more power to you. You know what you're paying for. You're paying for convenience, and you're good with that. You are likely not the employer complaining about their benefits expenditure or employees' view of your offerings.

But, if you are not intentionally choosing inertia, then you have no choice but to re-evaluate what you've been doing (or not doing) and why. Few of us business owners became entrepreneurs simply so we could craft and maintain a benefits plan. Yet, we find ourselves tasked with creating benefit plans that retract and retain talent we can afford. It feels almost hopeless. It is virtually impossible to know whom you should listen to as you try to discern who you can trust.

For the sake of this chapter, let's pretend you have figured out what is best for your health plan, that you've vetted all the options, and identified the right vendors and solutions. That is honestly only the first half of the battle.

The next obstacle is managing the change. That change is a hill many do not want to climb. The health plan that your employees and their families heavily rely on has likely become very personal for them. If (and when) you make dramatic changes to their benefits, they will not only notice but react and maybe even panic. That shouldn't dissuade you from making the necessary systemic improvements because there are many effective ways to manage this. Assuming you have a solution and vendor vetting process, you should have a change management process.

When I first learned of Kurt Lewin's Change Theory from the 1940s, I was struck by its genius and universal applicability. I am constantly finding scenarios within the health industry where it would've been vital and could've prevented crisis and chaos. At its core, it's a simple three-step process to effectively managing change:

Step 1: Unfreeze

Step 2: Change

Step 3: Refreeze

All too often, we skip to the change step, paying little or no attention to unfreezing or refreezing. Think of the unfreezing/refreezing in the context of ice. Let's pretend you have ice that you've frozen into circular molds for a particular glass, but then you discover you needed them to be tall, skinny cubes for a bottle. To reshape the ice, you would have to unfreeze (melt) the ice and refreeze it into the new molds.

For the record, I doubt we would unfreeze the ice. Instead, we would dump them and use new water for the new cubes. While this isn't the point of this analogy or Lewin's Change Theory, it is also a nod to what is fundamentally wrong with how we tackle change in this industry. We don't unfreeze/refreeze—we scratch it and start something different. This approach is arguably as flawed as never changing.

First, let's examine unfreezing. This involves acknowledging that a change is necessary and finding the words and messaging to communicate why. We hear about it in marketing—speaking to the problem we solve for our customers or the gap we fill. We don't put the same effort into with change we are implementing for our employees. Unfreezing in the world of employee benefits looks like starting the conversation months before the annual renewal. It looks like honest dialogue with HR and Finance, and maybe even the entire employee population.

I've found the most effective way to unfreeze and communicate the "why" behind the need for change is to use what you already have at your disposal—what isn't working? What isn't working could be identified by the complaints employees have. It could be the brutal reality that you cannot afford to contribute the same percentage to their benefits if costs keep increasing. It could be the devastating truth that you will face a choice like layoffs or pay/hiring freezes. Or maybe you face turnover problems because people are going to your competitor because of the benefits.

Maybe you're not comfortable talking about the internal problems you have to solve. Then talk about the external truth—that healthcare and insurance are often corrupt, difficult to navigate, and immovable if you don't get control. You can't stay still, or you're moving backward. You can't let inertia be your primary force. The unfreezing stage may take months or even years. Some employers partner with their advisors for this, while others approach it with more questions than comments and ask for feedback from their employees about what is working and what isn't, regardless of *how* an unfreezing effort is necessary. You probably have a gut instinct on if this is something you do well as a company or not. How well did you manage the change if you've rolled out a new procedure, changed technology systems, or restructured?

The next step is the change itself. This is usually the step everyone skips to. Within the change stage, more is necessary than just change. Attention to the messaging of the change is vital. Even the timing requires attention. If you are making changes, sending a notification email or scheduling a company-wide meeting to announce the change probably isn't sufficient to get real adoption, buy-in, or support from employees (even if there's coffee and bagels). It's advised that you even select ambassadors within your company whom you've taken time to get up to speed on the change and who can genuinely help guide the tide throughout the change phase.

The final stage is refreezing, and although it is also often overlooked after the change, it is as crucial as the other stages. It is refreezing that ensures that the change actually sticks. Change is hard. Even when it's right. It's in our human nature to react to change with heightened sensitivity because we are looking out to see if we need to do anything different to protect ourselves. Executing well on unfreezing and change is wasted if there isn't adequate refreezing.

Lewin's Change Theory is about 80 years old but has incredible implications for today and this industry. Not only are the stages applicable, but he introduces concepts of "restraining forces" and "driving forces" as affecting change management. These are not unique to change management. In every business activity, restraining and driving forces come into effect. Restraining forces pull against the momentum of the change while driving forces accelerate toward change.

I've seen these forces in the form of departments, initiatives, campaigns, or specific people. Specific people are an essential part of the process and will fall somewhere on the spectrum from restraining to driving. Change will show a side of your people you may not have seen before (hopefully for the better). Managing the change is crucial if you're changing your network, pharmacy vendor, carrier, or funding mechanism. Paying attention to how everyone shows up gives you valuable insight into your people. Do you have people in leadership restraining the change when they shouldn't? Are there people acting as driving forces or hidden leaders you hadn't noticed before?

I have countless stories of companies making the right changes but doing it the wrong way. The collateral damage is that the change itself is seen as the problem when it could have simply been the flawed execution. It also creates a traumatic response to future changes that need to be implemented. Since a prior change failed, folks are nervous to try it again—even if it's the right change.

A company that went self-funded and had a negligent TPA with poor customer service stays fully insured because they see all self-funding as too difficult to handle.

A group plan who forewent a national provider network for a more localized approach refuses to consider anything but the big national PPOs because the local option was newer and had growing pains at launch. These entities didn't necessarily make the wrong change, they managed it poorly, and the aftermath followed them.

Since there are so many considerations here, you can't help but ask if you have the right partners walking through the change stages with you. Is your broker someone who understands that change requires intentional, well-developed stages? Or do they provide you with a spreadsheet or proposal showing you a handful of options and asking you which one to pick? Are they actively involved in the unfreezing stage itself? Are they willing to humble themselves enough to recognize that what you have now may not be working and they may need to change themselves? What if your change requires significant work for them? Does it change the way they respond?

These are the technical considerations you need to make to fight inertia, discover the change you need to make, and efficiently implement it. Maybe you haven't invested the time and energy into managing the change the way you could have. But what else is holding you back? What's stopping you from changing and keeping you stuck with the inertia of it all? Let's look at the definition again with this in mind:

"A property of matter by which it continues in its existing state of rest or uniform motion in a straight line unless an external force changes that state."

Every employer must answer this fundamental question—is your benefits plan at rest or in motion?

I'm not advocating change for change's sake. I'm simply reporting on what I've seen in my time in this industry with hundreds of employers. Part of what leads to the inertia and resistance to significant change is a lack of purpose or direction for the benefits program itself.

If a company is checking a box to meet legal and regulatory obligations, that's ok—there are still some self-reflective questions to ask. Within that box-checking exercise, what are your priorities?

- Keeping costs as low as humanly possible no matter what?
- Balancing cost with employee experience?
- Offering the richest benefits you can afford?

If a company wants more from their benefits and sees it as a vision-affirming opportunity for its employees, there are even more questions to ask to determine the real goal.

Do you fundamentally believe your employees should be engaged consumers in the process, or are you looking to do it all for them? Are you willing to pay for convenience? Is cost your only motivator?

I'm reminded of an early client I had back when "Cadillac" plans were all the buzz. They said, "we don't have Cadillac employees; we don't need a Cadillac plan." No judgment here. You know your company, people, vision, and budget. But it would serve you well to consider those variables when you consider your plan, what changes might need to be made, and on what timeline you are making them.

I will not lie to you—doing the work I'm talking about here and then implementing whatever changes you deem necessary will not be easy or fast. Shit will still break. You are not in control of healthcare in America. Vendors, providers, members, etc., are all playing this multi-player game you are paying for. You cannot control all the moving parts or prevent things from going wrong. You are only in control of what you offer, how you implement it, how you maintain it, how you respond when things break, and who you take along for the ride with you. You must be willing to call an audible when necessary or regroup if things aren't working.

Speaking of calling an audible, I am not a sports connoisseur, much to my husband's chagrin. He was/is a die-hard Peyton Manning fan. We followed as loyal fans from the Colts to the Broncos. I remember watching Colts games and not understanding why we would continue to call and attempt to run plays when we were repeatedly getting zero yards. I couldn't watch it; it was too frustrating. You sports fans probably have games, players, plays, etc., that infuriate you. As a spectator, you see the alternate "right" approach. We are all great armchair quarterbacks, I'm sure. While my husband would laugh at me and my unreasonable irritation, he would explain how the vantage point is so different when you're on the field running with the ball. The great running backs "see the holes," but not everyone does because they aren't as clear from the field as they are on your TV or stadium seats.

So, as you consider your relationship with inertia, the stages of change, and any restraining or driving forces, also consider your vantage point. You're the Joseph Addai of my story (former Colts running back whose name I only knew because it seemed like every time I was yelling at the TV about a run play, he had the ball and was spinning). We are all sitting back at home watching.

So, what can you do to shake up your vantage point? If it's too close to home, bring an outsider in. Not your current broker or your current HR Manager. An outsider. Look at what your competitors are doing. Ask questions in your exit interviews with employees leaving. Talk to your employees (and their spouses!) about the health plan. Review publicly available benchmarking data to see how you stack up. Compare what you're doing now to what you did five years ago. Articulate a vision for your benefits plan and set tangible goals with timelines.

Then look around and determine who should be with you for that ride. You probably wouldn't hire a rep from a bookkeeping software company to run your accounting department because they could get you the best deal with the software. You probably wouldn't hire an otherwise unqualified Auto Zone employee to maintain your fleet of vehicles because you get a discount on parts. Don't make that mistake with your broker. Identify your vision first. Then decide whom you want to help you drive the change it will take to get you there. Gather all the facts you need. Be prepared so that it won't look like inertia's straight line.

Then go. Forward is a direction.

CONTRIBUTORS

BLAKE ALLISON. Blake serves as chief executive officer of Employers Health Network, responsible for the overall strategic direction and performance of the company. He is focused on advancing the company's mission of aligning high-performing, integrated delivery systems for employers to drive innovation and high-value healthcare. Prior to joining EHN, Blake served as the CEO of Southeastern Health Partners, a clinically integrated network between three delivery systems with over 2,000 providers and over 75,000 covered lives, as well as COO of the Baylor Scott & White Quality Alliance. Blake's experience spans multiple settings, from physician consulting to large integrated delivery systems in various parts of the country.
Blake received a Bachelor of Science in Education from Baylor University and a Master of Science in Healthcare Administration from Trinity University.

PAUL CARTER. Paul has spent the better part of three decades in the healthcare industry, the last 25 years on the payer side. He has significant experience in both the fully insured business and health plan administration for self-funded employer groups. Paul's knowledge and experience allow him to look at healthcare from both the insurance company/administration perspective as well as the employer's perspective. Paul Carter is a nationally recognized leader in innovative health plan design and cost containment models.

TOM DILIEGRO. Tom graduated from Merrimack College with a BS in Health Science and Chemistry. Intending to pursue a career as a physician, life circumstances intervened, and he was taken in another direction. He moved South in 2003 and received an MBA from the Citadel. In 2007, he was hired at a BCBS-owned TPA, where he became an expert in account-based plans and self-funding. In 2013, he was hired by Roper St. Francis Healthcare in the Managed Care department, where he managed a private-label health plan and negotiated and executed managed care contracts. In 2017, after a decade of payer and facility experience, Tom became an advocate for the employer. He hung a shingle full-time as Benefit Advisors of Charleston, now known as Vero Advising. Tom lives in Charleston, SC. He is married to Amy and has four kids, a dog, and seven chickens.

ERIKA ENSIGN. Erika began her insurance career in 2010 on the carrier side. By 2013, she transitioned to the agency side of the industry to make a greater impact on employers. Erika's uncompromising approach to challenging the status quo in the complex world of employee benefits helps her create ways to maximize the employer's dollars while improving employee experience. Erika graduated from Texas A&M University-Commerce in 2008 and 2010 earning both bachelor's and master's degrees in Health and Wellness. She was born and raised in Houston, Texas. Erika and her husband live in Pearland, Texas, with their children. Her hobbies include traveling, reading, and working out.

HILARY GERAGHTY. Hilary is a well-known underwriter and respected "rainmaker" in the medical stop-loss and reinsurance industry. Hilary started Tactical Reinsurance MGU (www.TacticalReinsurance.com) to make an impactful difference to all that is wrong with healthcare and the employee benefits delivery market. The driving force behind her ambitious journey is her two-year-old daughter. The best way a mother can raise a daughter is through example, and Hilary lives a life of leadership, determination, and sincerity to help others.

TRENT HARPER. Trent started out as a runner at an insurance agency in Las Vegas, NV, while still in high school. Through various name changes and acquisitions, that company is now Breckpoint. Trent has eight years in the captive insurance industry, primarily at the executive level, on top of over fifteen years of experience in the alternative risk insurance market across employee benefits and property casualty lines of business. He is currently serving as president of Breckpoint, part of the Acrisure family. Trent specializes in finding creative solutions using alternative risk financing strategies across all lines of coverage with a particular focus on medical stop-loss and corresponding cost containment strategies. If he is not listening to some podcast, you will most likely find Trent with his wife and three kids living life.

AMY HOWARD. Amy has never been accused of being subtle. She has spent twenty-plus years in the insurance industry in the stop-loss arena. Most of her career has been with a national TPA working on everything from marketing, reporting, auditing, administration, and dabbling in licensure. She recently joined the carrier world at Breckpoint, Inc., where she has helped build a successful block of business alongside some top industry names. Outside of insurance, Amy is a proud mother of four who enjoys spending time reading psychological thrillers and watching Disney movies.

RACHEL MINER. Ever since she was little, Rachel believed in holding steadfast in doing the right thing and advocating for those who can't advocate for themself. She has won Rising Star in Benefits (2018, *Employee Benefit Advisor* magazine), Top Women in Benefits Advising (2020, *Employee Benefit Advisor* magazine), she was runner up for Broker of the Year (2021, *Employee Benefit Advisor* magazine). In addition, she was invited to the White House to discuss ways in which to lower RX in 2019. She also is very active in the National Association of Health Underwriters (NAHU).

DR. KRISTINE REGNIER, ND. Krissy grew up listening to her physician father speak to the misaligned motives of the healthcare system. As a result, she became a champion of uncovering and addressing the underlying cause of chronic disease at an early age. Dr. Regnier holds a doctorate in Naturopathic Medicine with over eight years of experience working with employers to develop programs to manage the health of their workforce. Specific areas include crafting alternative benefit structures, occupational health, wellness, and prevention. Dr. Regnier can be found hiking the trails in Northwest Indiana, which she calls home with her husband and two stepchildren.

SPENCER SMITH. As senior vice president of sales for Plansight, Spencer has over fifteen years of insurance industry experience, with the last eight years focused on self-funding, stop-loss insurance, and insurance technology (InsureTech). In 2020 he produced a series of whiteboard videos on stop-loss insurance that benefits agencies across the country have used to train their staff and have amassed over 25,000 views on YouTube. He also hosts a video podcast called "Self-Funded with Spencer," which features self-funded industry thought leaders and is considered one of the top podcasts in the entire insurance industry. Spencer loves soccer, heavy metal, Roush mustangs, and most of all, his wife Courtney and two children, Brooklyn, 5, and Sebastian, 2.

DOUG SHERMAN. Doug was CEO, founder, and co-founder of several high-growth companies following his service as an Air Force fighter pilot instructor. His first company, DSG Consulting, served 150 companies in thirty countries, including Boeing Commercial Aircraft, GE, Siemens, and more. Currently, Doug and his son own an ecosystem of health insurance companies, a health insurance agency, Clearwater Benefits, a TPA Clearwater Benefits Administrator, and facilitated the founding of ClearShare, a medical cost-sharing organization non-profit. He has authored eight books, including *Your Work Matters to God*. Doug Sherman is a graduate of the United States Air Force Academy and holds a B.S. in Engineering Management.

RACHEL STRAUSS. Nicknamed the PBM Princess, Rachel has more than twenty years under her tiara as part of the insurance industry. As the Vice President of Business Development for EHIM, she uniquely began in pharmacy underwriting. Rachel has spent the last few years focused on education, speaking engagements, and helping promote dialogue within the industry. In addition, Rachel is dedicated to the philanthropic world. She finds volunteerism and giving back to be one of the most fulfilling parts of her life. When Rachel is not amongst the PBM Kingdom, she can be found spending time with her husband, Levi, and two young children, Leo and Goldie.

ACKNOWLEDGMENTS

Ten years ago, when I was deep in the throws of non-profit work, marketing, and event planning, I never would've imagined this is where I would be today. A passion for health insurance operations was not a jewel in any crown I imagined for my life. But here we are. And I can't fight it. My career and this anthology were not a feat of my own; rather, it took a village that I'd be remiss not to acknowledge.

First, to my contributors:

Dr. Kristine Regnier: You are a force to be reckoned with. The healthcare industry, and now the insurance service industry, have been so lucky to have you. After everything we've been through together, learning and growing alongside you is still a blast. Your dedication to caring for the people in this world is something I respect so much. Stay honest and bold. Don't let this industry kill your voice or fire for change.

Blake Allison: Our fired-up chats about providers and payers and everything that's broken about our industry have taught me so much. The work you and EHN do is changing the world; I'm convinced of it as I've seen it firsthand. I know it can sometimes be discouraging to feel like you know or have the secret sauce, but the world isn't getting it. I'm glad you guys don't give up and are changing how employers and employees access QUALITY healthcare. You and your team have taught me so much, and I'm grateful to work with you. Thank you for bringing your message to this book.

Tom DiLiegro: It feels like yesterday we began our work together. One of the great honors of presenting this anthology has been bringing the untold stories of true visionaries forward. Yours is one of those. I am so glad that despite the corruption and disheartening rules of engagement that you've encountered in this industry, you push on. Your clients, your community, and the larger world are lucky to have you doing the good work for all the right reasons. Your dad would be proud.

Erika Ensign: Girl. Look what we've done together and in support of each other in just a few short years! You are taking the world by storm. Your authenticity and dedication to your clients is a truly remarkable thing. It means the world to me to have your insights in this book. Our partnership through the years has kept my hope alive that all is not lost in this business and that there are still some good ones doing good things. Thank you for being the light to so many. YAMFC.

Rachel Strauss: I still laugh when I think that I almost didn't talk to you when we first met. I just couldn't consider that maybe not all PBMs were evil. I'm glad I listened; glad I opened my mind enough to let you teach me everything you have over the years. You are truly the PBM princess, and I can't imagine navigating the pharmacy world without you. Your friendship and support have helped guide me through some difficult career challenges. I only hope I can bring as much support to you as you have to me. I'm grateful you were bold enough to tell your truth in this book. The world needs to hear it. You and EHIM are the good ones.

Paul Carter: Feels like yesterday that I talked so much shit about TPAs on stage at an industry conference, and then you got on stage next! I remember being mortified and intrigued about someone who spoke the truth about the world from the TPA seat. The rest is history. Who knew years later I would revere you as the TPA Godfather? Your leadership in the space is more than guiding TPA practices—you have mentored, coached, and led so many of us that your impact is felt everywhere. I can't thank you enough for your truth in this book, your work in the space, and the time and energy you've invested in me and others who want to change the industry for the better. You're a visionary.

Spencer Smith: Your podcast has been a light in this industry as you teach and entertain. It is refreshing to work with folks who desire to learn and grow and then pay it forward. I knew that was you from the beginning. Your experience and expertise are remarkable, and it was an honor to have your words on these pages. Thank you for doing the good work.

Rachel Miner: I hate that you and your family went through what you did, but our readers are lucky to learn from it. I'm glad this industry hasn't scarred you too badly, and you are bold enough to share your message. Thanks for being a part of this project and your work in this field!

Hilary Geraghty: The world needs more women underwriters! Watching what you've accomplished in the space has been fun and brings promise to a sometimes-depressing industry. I'm so thrilled that you told the truth in the way you did in this book and exemplified thought leadership in a way so many are too afraid to. I can't wait to be along for the ride to watch everything you accomplish in your career!

Trent Harper: I don't know that many if any, understand stop-loss and captives as well as you. If I can do anything to expand your reach or elevate your message, it is an honor to do so because of the integrity you exemplify. The world needs more creative, truthful leaders in the space, and your leadership and progressive but thoughtful delivery are vital. I'm grateful for your time and energy in teaching me and others and crafting effective, sustainable offerings for employers.

Amy Howard: My only wish is that we'd met each other sooner! Working with you has been fun and enlightening. I said it—you make underwriting and stop-loss fun. We are lucky to have your insights and truth about what works and what we need to think about. I'm so grateful that you were part of this project and honored to get to elevate your message and experience.

Doug Sherman: I have somehow found myself lucky enough to be in your ecosystem. You have left your imprint on so many individuals and businesses in so many industries. Your leadership with clients, mentorship, and strategic insights are welcome to the healthcare and insurance industries. We are honored to have your leadership on these pages and in the industry.

To my remarkable mentors and partners in business, entrepreneur-ship, and life... Mindi Fynke, Carrie Urbanelli, Shawn Evans, Steve

Butz (and the Certus team), Tom Walaszek (and the Accurisk team), Dr. Christine Whitaker, Sunny Nadolsky, Kevin Brown, Levi Strauss, Jason Sherman, Don Collis, Collin Bryce, Matt Downs, Cary Barr, and Larry Hunter-Blank.

I know you weren't able to be a part of this project, but you all exemplify supreme integrity, genuine goodness, and extraordinary authenticity. The world and the larger business community are better for having each of you and your companies in it. You each inspired this work, and your support and encouragement through the process were more appreciated than you will ever know.

Jill Carlyle, my fantastic publisher and friend. Thank you for taking a chance on me and this exposé of sorts. Your faith in me and the project mean more to me than you know! I am grateful for the time, energy, and resources you spent on this project and the vision and mission you're pursuing with The Empowered Press. You are changing the world, and I am honored to be a part of it.

To the women who I've met (and those I haven't), who have overcome the obstacles of this industry and paved the way for so many of us.

To the women who will come after us. May you feel empowered and supported enough to speak the truth and be boldly yourself, making your own lasting imprint on the industry.

To my mother, Jackie, and sister Hannah, who have always been my editors and cheerleaders, always in my corner, reminding me I can accomplish anything.

To my godfather Pierre, who has shown me what persistence, passion, and peace look like in this world.

To Grandpa Millard and Grandma Pat (rest in peace), who showed me unconditional love, a virtual cloak of invincibility, and showed me the life I wanted to build is possible if I do the work and am willing to listen to those who know better than I do.

My husband, Scottie, and my sons: I could not have done this without your patience and unconditional love. You make me braver. Babe, thanks for always pushing me and reminding me that nothing counts if it's not built on truth and integrity. Thank you for never letting me give in to the temptation to mute myself, compromise my values, or settle for what the world says a woman should accomplish in this space. Boys, I know this project took me from you for a while. I hate that, but I also want you to see that the things that make a difference in the world take work and sacrifice. I can't wait to see what imprint the three of you leave on this world.

ABOUT THE PRESENTER

Photo by: Helms Photography

Dr. Madeline Smith is the Founder and CEO of MADDRS, LLC (pronounced "matters"). Madeline earned her Bachelor of Arts in Religious Studies and Philosophy and holds an MBA and a Doctorate in Business Administration, where her research examined the role of corporate social responsibility in the health insurance industry. After more than seven years of working in nonprofit administration and strategic planning as VP of Development and Marketing, she felt the desire to make an impact in the insurance, healthcare, and risk management industry. Her work has been exclusively in the self-funded arena, overseeing operations, underwriting, and marketing & sales as the Chief Growth Officer of a domestic health captive and brokerage agency.

In 2019, Dr. Smith started an independent business coaching and operations consulting firm supporting service providers, consultants, captives, carriers, and networks. Madeline works to stand out in the industry, being able to bring together like-minded entities around phenomenally different solutions with an ability to see the big picture. She makes it her business to effectively manage the minutia and keep focused on the people and families at the center of it all. She aims to be known by her colleagues and clients as a truth-teller who has a reputation for making a difference and promoting programs she stands 100 percent behind.

Smith is a lifelong learner. Currently, she is a JD Candidate at St. Mary's School of Law. When she's not working or studying, she spends time with her husband and three sons, writing something, or on an outdoor run planning her next project.

MOFO THE MOVEMENT...

BECAUSE CHANGING AMERICAN HEALTHCARE WILL TAKE MORE THAN BOOKS

It will take more than podcasts, articles, social media, exposes, and even government regulations.

It will take all of us coming together—people of all economic backgrounds, politics, gender, race, and health status…

To acknowledge that access to affordable health care is a basic human right. The uniform goal of the movement is to make health and wellness an affordable reality for all Americans rather than a corrupt system bankrolling a few to the detriment of the many.

It begins with unbiased truth, facts, and guidance to inform choice and empower individuals to make sense of it all and know how to navigate the system.

Let's connect.

For more information, scan the QR code, or email us:

info@mofothemovement.com

mofothemovement.com